KKKTa9: 851 40

SOCIAL DANCE

from *Dance A While*

SECOND EDITION

Jane A. Harris

Anne M. Pittman

Marlys S. Waller

Cathy L. Dark

You Save $ At
Student Bookstore
3002 Ayers at Edwards

D0160930

Benjamin
Cummings

San Francisco   Boston   New York
Cape Town   Hong Kong   London   Madrid   Mexico City
Montreal   Munich   Paris   Singapore   Sydney   Tokyo   Toronto

Publisher: Daryl Fox
Acquisitions Editor: Deirdre McGill
Publishing Assistant: Michelle Cadden
Managing Editor: Wendy Earl
Production Editor: Michele Mangelli
Copyeditor: Sally Peyrefitte
Cover design: Yvo Riezebos
Composition: Greene Design
Manufacturing Buyer: Stacey Weinberger
Marketing Manager: Sandra Lindelof

Library of Congress Cataloging–in–Publication Data

Social dance : from Dance a while / Jane A. Harris ... [et al.].—2nd ed.
     p. cm.
     Rev. ed. of Social dance / Jane A. Harris, Anne M. Pittman, Marlys S. Waller. c1998.
     Includes bibliographical references and index.
     ISBN 0-8053-5366-6 (soft cover)
     1. Ballroom dancing—Study and teaching. I. Harris, Jane A. II. Harris, Jane A. Social
dance. III. Dance a while.

GV1753.5 .H37 2002
793.3'3'07–dc21

2002073361

Copyright © 2003 Pearson Education, Inc., publishing as Benjamin Cummings,
1301 Sansome St., San Francisco, CA 94111. All rights reserved. Manufactured in
the United States of America. This publication is protected by Copyright and
permission should be obtained from the publisher prior to any prohibited
reproduction, storage in a retrieval system, or transmission in any form or by
any means, electronic, mechanical, photocopying, recording, or likewise. To
obtain permission(s) to use material from this work, please submit a written
request to Pearson Education, Inc., Permission Department, 1900 E. Lake Ave.,
Glenview, IL 60025. For information regarding permissions, call (847) 486-2635.

Many of the designations used by manufacturers and sellers to distinguish their
products are claimed as trademarks. Where those designations appear in this
book, and the publisher was aware of a trademark claim, the designations have
been printed in initial caps or all caps.

ISBN 0-8053-5366-6
2 3 4 5 6 7 8 9 10–BAH–06 05 04 03 02
www.aw.com/bc

TABLE OF CONTENTS

Chapter 1   Introduction to Social Dance

Chapter 2   Ballroom Favorites

Chapter 3   Swing (Jitterbug)

Chapter 6   Latin Dances

Chapter 7   Mixers and Ice Breakers

FOREWORD

The authors are at it again, bringing out this timely edition of *Social Dance* in response to the reappearance of big bands and pop groups with Swing, Country Western, Rock, and even the Latin rhythms.

I was captivated recently when a former student invited me to visit her middle school Holiday Dance. I saw 400 students fill the dance floor—in small groups, singles and in couples, having great fun dancing and singing to pop music. They had picked up on these catchy, clever movements in class the previous weeks, and everyone wanted to be a part of the fun.

New, elegant recreation centers on college campuses are drawing thousands of students around the clock in search of fitness, getting acquainted and participating socially. Dance has a prominent place in this setting—dance classes are even offered and filled.

It is evident that dance brings cultures together. It is a language that everyone understands. Teachers and leaders in all settings are eager for new ideas and guidance in working effectively to make the social occasion enjoyable for all, and *Social Dance* provides these ideas.

The authors of *Social Dance* are to be congratulated on bringing the social dance section of *Dance A While* out in a separate volume. Teachers and leaders will be delighted with this guide to new materials, and detailed directions and leadership techniques for promoting social dance as it grows and changes.

For many years as co-authors of *Dance A While*, I worked with Marlys Waller and Anne Pittman. I am so proud of their continuing contribution to the field of dance and I am most happy to recommend this new volume.

Jane Harris Ericson

PREFACE

Social dance is the most popular recreational dance of all. People move, wiggle, and snap to the beat of the music they hear on the radio, television, videos, wedding celebrations, and family gatherings. From solo to partners, young to old, people learn to move in response to the Foxtrot, Waltz, Latin, Hustle, Country, and Contemporary music as a dance activity. The opportunity to meet new people, to socialize, to court, to celebrate are all a part of the social dance scene.

This new edition of *Social Dance* includes extensive new material. Swing is given its due as a whole chapter, along with many new variations and in depth material on the Lindy Hop has been added.

Separated from the eighth edition of *Dance A While*, *Social Dance* offers a focused package for just social dance instruction—the traditional Ballroom Favorites, Swing, Country Western, Line Dances, and a "fun lovin'" chapter of golden oldie Mixers and Ice Breakers are included.

Cathy L. Dark adds her expertise to our latest edition. Cathy is on the faculty at Oregon State University, and teaches Ballroom and Country Western Dance. She is an advisor to "Cool Shoes," the Oregon State University Ballroom Performing Group.

Social Dance is designed for the teacher and student of ballroom instruction, whether in the college setting, activity center, family room, or dance studio. It is an excellent reference of variations, forever useful.

Dance like nobody's watching! Enjoy! We pass this wondrous tradition on to those of you who "gotta dance"!

■ *Acknowledgments*

During 48 years of publication it has been our custom to research and write a different section with each revision of *Dance A While*. *Social Dance* from *Dance A While* is a spin–off of materials found in the social dance section of the main text. We would like to express our great appreciation to our former co–author and colleague, Jane A. Harris (Ericson), for her extensive work in developing the format and content of this section.

In addition to the materials from the eighth edition, we have been fortunate recipients of materials from Kathy DuBois of the University of Wisconsin, La Crosse; Gary E. Sanders of the University of Missouri, Kansas City; and longtime friend, Henry "Buzz" Glass.

Social Dance from *Dance A While* inherits all the grass roots research and enthusiasm the authors have put into all previous editions. We hope this second edition of *Social Dance* will make a solid contribution to the longevity of the present popularity and enthusiasm for ballroom and other social dancing.

Anne M. Pittman
Marlys S. Waller
Cathy L. Dark

INTRODUCTION *to* SOCIAL DANCE

Dance and music are not static forms. They mirror the culture in which they exist by reflecting the past, present, and any intercultural exchanges that have occurred. The everchanging human scene is absorbed and acted out in dance and music forms.

The Renaissance of the fifteenth and sixteenth century in Italy and France saw the rebirth of interest in learning, literature, arts, and creative expression in general. The invention of printing made it possible for dance instruction and music notation to be widely distributed. Avid interest in dance and the creation of new musical forms swept through the courts of Europe. The period saw the establishment of dance teaching as a profession. New court dances were developed by professionals for the nobility. Courts used dance as an opportunity to educate courtiers in social graces and deportment. Queen Elizabeth established social dance as an important part of court life. English country dance began to appear in court, and English dancing schools were in vogue. Dances in the latter part of Queen Elizabeth's reign were gay, lively, and extremely popular.

The first half of the sixteenth century (1500–1550) saw the Basse dance reign as queen of the dance along with caroles, pavanes and turgions. During the last half (1550–1600) brawls (branle), rounds, heys, ring dances, galliards, courantores, La Voltas and allemandes were the dances of the day. Dancing became an everyday adjunct to court life in the palaces of the Renaissance.

In Colonial America, military balls and elaborate cotillions were popular. The hearty pioneers brought dance to the taverns and public dance halls with their western migration. In more modern times, college proms and special festive occasions were the impetus for social dancing. Night clubs became the ballrooms for the dancing public. Clubs often specialized in a particular type of dance such as Country Western Swing of one variety or the other, Latin, or simply an evening of ballroom favorites danced to the "big band" sound. Social Dance has always been a viable part of the social life in America.

■ *Phases of Social Dance*

Since the 1900s, eight periods have marked the progress of Social Dance, and each was stimulated or motivated by a new style of music. The *Foxtrot* had its beginnings in the early 1900s as a fast trotting step to a new jazz called "ragtime." Novelty dances like the Bunny Hug and the Grizzly Bear were widely popular during World War I. Next came Dixieland jazz and an athletic dance called the Charleston. Although a strenuous dance done to a syncopated beat, it found great favor among those sporting the "flap-per style" of dress and look of the Roaring Twenties.

From the 1930s to the 1950s, big band music produced hundreds of tunes that have become classics. The *Lindy*, also called jitterbug and later Swing, made its appearance. Big band music changed the Foxtrot into a smooth dance with many variations. Even the Waltz took on a new, more sophisticated look. The Big Apple, Shag, and Lambeth Walk were the main dance interest of the college crowd. The popularity of dancing to big band music increased the need for and the number of dance studios. The swinging and swaying of big band music also gave rise to large public ballrooms across the country. Although the Swing faded with the demise of the big bands, it returned in the 1980s and 1990s to be danced to a variety of rhythm styles of the period.

The *Tango* was a fad during the 1920s and has remained a ballroom favorite over the years, although at times overshadowed by interest in other Latin dances. Stimulated by an influx of Latin music, the Cuban Rumba started a new trend toward Latin dances in the 1930s. The Brazilian Samba, Mambo, Cha Cha Cha, Calypso, Merengue, and later the Bossa Nova all enjoyed brief but exciting periods of popularity. The Tango, however, has endured as a ballroom favorite.

The beat and sound decibels produced by rock music demanded a dance response that was to characterize the period during and after World War II. Rock and roll was the music of such legends as Elvis Presley, the Beatles, Rolling Stones, and the Beach Boys. Dance movement became unencumbered by pattern or partner except as the dance action was performed facing and gyrating with another person. Dance bands and dance floor space became smaller. Disc jockeys and recorded music became the norm. Novelty or fad dances such as the Twist, Slop, Mashed Potato, Swim, Monkey, Pony, Bug, Hitch Hiker, Watusi, Hully Gully, and Jerk enjoyed various degrees and length of popularity. Television and videos became the major vehicles for disseminat-ing rock and roll music, dance, manners, and dress.

Country Western had its roots in the music and songs brought by European immi-grants to the Appalachian Mountains in the Eastern United States. The mix of people from this region with a wider spectrum of people during World War II led to an explo-sion of interest in the music and songs of these mountain people. Songs and music of the cowboys from Texas and the Southwest had generally become entrenched after the Civil War. These two music and dance forms coupled with the adaptation of western cowboy dress became what is now known as Country Western. Country Western radio stations have long enjoyed popularity with a loyal listening public.

Swing, Disco Swing, and Country Swing are the basic patterns used in dancing to Country Western music. Line dancing has emerged to take its place alongside Country Western dance. Both enjoy a wide following and are danced to the same music at the same time. While couples dance in the line of direction around the dance floor, line dancers carry on in the center moving forward and back or sideways without interfer-ing with the traditional flow of dancers around the perimeter.

From the inner cities comes Street dance. Break dancing and Hip Hop have roots in African American culture. Break dancing is an acrobatic form coming out of New York's south Bronx. Hip Hop has its roots in rap, but also embraces soul, funk, jazz, and dance hall reggae. The accompanying music is electronic funk with a machine-gun style chanting called rap.

■ *Competition*

Competition has long been a part of the history of ballroom dance. In England an Open Foxtrot Competition was held in 1920. It was so successful that a later event, the Ivory Cross Competition, featured "heats" held in various provincial centers and in London. Dance teams thus qualified for the Grand Finals, which were held in December of 1921. The success of this type of qualifying led to the first national competition sponsored by the *Daily Sketch*, a London newspaper. In 1922 England held its first major competition to determine the best "all–rounder." Teams competed in three dances: the Waltz, Foxtrot, and One–Step.

The success of these early events led to many big ballroom championships and competitions throughout England well into the 1950s. The Star Championship held since 1920 terminated in the '50s but was replaced in 1953 by the International Championships held at Albert Hall in London. The latter continues to this day. Undoubtedly the most famous British competition is the internationally renowned Blackpool Dance Festival begun in 1930. This renowned festival draws dancers from around the world and is open to professionals and amateurs alike. Thousands of couples from all over the world convened at the 1998 Blackpool Festival. Some 75 couples from North America competed in one or more competitions. The United States is reported to have enjoyed unprecedented success with the Brigham Young University team securing wins in both the Ballroom and Latin Formation Championships in what is an exclusively amateur division.

In the United States the major venues for ballroom dance competition are the hundreds of dance competitions held annually across the country. In the early 1930s the Harvest Moon Hall was a major venue and at its height in the 1940s was a dance classic!

Of major importance at present is the Ohio Star Ball that began as a one–day event in 1977 designed to attract dancers from the immediate area. Its success led to a two–day and later a three–day competition in the late '70s. By the mid '80s entries had grown from 3,000 to 10,000. Billed as the Championship Ballroom Dance, the Ohio Star Ball has been televised by the Public Broadcasting System (PBS) since 1987. The viewership is reported to have increased from 9 million in 1991 to more than 13 million at the present. The Ohio Star Ball is a monumental dance spectacular celebrating its 20th anniversary.

In the past decade both amateur and professional dancers have been entering contests in record numbers. The United States Amateur Ballroom Dance Association sponsors a network of contests and reports a rapid rise in member organization from 15 to 40 in the late 1990s. Other major competitions are the United States Ballroom Championships and the Imperial Society of Teachers of Dance. These venues plus hundreds of regional competitions make the ballroom scene one of beauty, skill, and exciting action enjoyed by dancer and spectator alike.

Competitive ballroom dance, whether for the amateur or professional, is a tough world. In a major division, for example, up to 50 couples may be selected from successive rounds lasting less than two minutes. Final selection may then be made from as few as six couples. Judges look for timing, rhythm, hip movements, head control, accuracy of footwork, and the level of difficulty of the routine. These determinations are made in two major divisions: Latin, which includes rumba, samba, cha–cha–cha, paso doble, jive, and Modern, which includes waltz, tango, foxtrot, quick step, and Viennese waltz. Couples may compete as a amateur, professional, or pro–am status. Although some compete only in one form, many compete in all 10 forms.

Public awareness of ballroom dance has come about through the influence of a number of factors. Ice–dancing uses ballroom dance forms, as does the skating in Ice Capades. Television, of course, has played an enormous role. Observances such as Ballroom Dance, sponsored by the New York Mayor's Office, and a move by Alabama dancers to have their senator help establish a National Ballroom Dance Week help build enthusiasm. College and university campuses have shown renewed interest in ballroom dance. Brigham Young University sports the largest ballroom dance program in the country along with a touring performance group that travels and performs internationally. Other active centers are Wisconsin, Texas, University of California at Berkeley, and New York University. Several have very active dance teams. The attraction of ballroom dance seems to be that it allows a certain intimacy that produces a sense of pride, resulting in greater self–assurance for participants. This is in contrast to the solo type performance of rock and roll.

The reemergence of "touch dancing," or ballroom forms of the early 1900s, seems refreshing and widely welcomed. The likelihood, however, of its comeback matching its earlier popularity depends upon two circumstances: composers writing music for this type of dance and space to accommodate large groups of dancers. In earlier times there were major ballrooms, such as Roseland and the Rainbow Room in New York, especially designed for large crowds. At present there are no great moves by composers or promoters to support the renewed interest in these earlier dance forms.

■ *Dancesport*

Dancesport is the term given to ballroom dance competition held in the Olympics. It combines the theatrical performance elements of the activity with the aura of a sport. Like swimming, wind surfing, and ice skating, dancesport is an extension of a widely popular recreational activity.

The International Olympic Committee (IOC) provisionally recognized dancesport in June 1995 and gave it full Olympic status in 1998. The International Dance Sports Federation (IDSF) is a nonprofit, nonpolitical organization, founded in 1957, that controls 95 percent of all international competitions, including granting of events governed by IDSF rules. The International Body of Dance Teachers and Promoters controls the remaining group of fully professional dancers.

The worldwide flavor and involvement in IDSF is demonstrated by the fact that between general meetings the affairs are conducted by a presidium composed of members from Germany, Australia, England, Denmark, Japan, Switzerland, Scotland, Russia, and the United States. The formation of the IDSF has greatly increased the interest in dancesport throughout the world. Membership at present consists of 64 countries from five continents. The World Rock 'n' Roll Confederation (WRRC) is an associate member representing some 30 countries.

The five dances used in dancesport competition are: the Modern Waltz, Tango, Viennese Waltz, Slow Foxtrot, and Quickstep. All dances are performed by a couple using the closed hold position. Figures have been standardized and categorized into various levels for teaching. Vocabularies, techniques, rhythms, and tempos have been internationally agreed upon to make instruction uniform.

■ Vintage Dance

Dances through the ages have cast their spell. They are a part of the common culture and a heritage to be borrowed, shared, and recreated. Thus, it is not surprising that there is, at present, considerable interest in reconstructing the ballroom dances of the nineteenth and early twentieth centuries. Staging quadrilles, contras, waltzes, polkas, rags, and tangos provide a rich opportunity for research and recreation in the areas of costuming, makeup, lighting, sound, and expanding dance skills.

It appears, therefore, that dance and the music that influenced it have come full circle. Big bands and partner or "touch" dancing have reappeared. Live bands playing a variety of rhythms such as Foxtrot, Swing, Latin, Rock, and Jazz are back in demand. Variety in music spawns variety in dance forms. America is dancing, and dancing in style!

TEACHING SOCIAL DANCE

Dealing effectively with inherent variables such as class size, available space, length of unit, and materials to be taught is of prime importance to both the teaching and learning processes. The following teaching techniques should be used carefully in relation to these variables.

■ Formations

The line, single line facing one direction or parallel lines with partner couples facing, is a highly effective formation to use in a social dance class. This formation allows students to see and hear the demonstration clearly. It also allows the teacher to face the class for explanations and turn his or her back to the class for demonstration purposes.

When there are two teachers, each can work with his or her back to a line in the parallel line formation. In the single line, couples may be side by side. In the parallel line, couples are opposite. The line formations are especially essential when teaching beginning steps.

■ Walk-Through

The teacher should be clearly seen and heard while demonstrating and analyzing the action of a step. On cue, the class should then follow through several times. The walk-through tempo should begin slowly and gradually increase until it is up to the tempo of the music to be used. The step should be tried first to music without a partner, then with a partner and music. A time free of instructional direction should be provided after the walk-through. During this time the teacher should circulate among the dancers giving individual assistance as needed.

■ The Cue

The whole principle of unison practice to develop rhythmic awareness is contingent upon the accuracy of a system of cueing. A signal, such as "ready and," serves to start the dancers in unison. It is important that the cues be given rhythmically! This helps the student to feel the timing. A variety of cues are used to help the student remember the foot pattern and rhythm. For example:

4/4	1–2	3	4
Rhythm cue:	slow	quick	quick
Step cue:	step	side	close
Direction cue:	turn	side	close
Style cue:	down	up	up
Warning cue: "get ready for the break"			
Foot cue:	right	left	right

A good technique is to change from one cue to the other as needed. Cueing is a help, not a crutch, and should be abandoned as soon as the students appear to be secure in their execution. Cueing at any stage in the learning process is best when done over a sound system that amplifies the voice.

■ Demonstration

The advantages of demonstration are (a) it hastens learning when students see what is to be learned, (b) it facilitates learning the style and flow of dance movement, and (c) teaching requires less talking, so that more practice is available. Demonstration is most helpful at the following times:

1. At the beginning of the lesson with partner and music to give a whole picture of the pattern. This is also a good motivational device.
2. When presenting a new step. Demonstrate the lead's and follow's parts separately, then the lead's as students take partners.
3. Demonstrate to teach style, the lead and follow relationships, and timing.
4. Occasionally demonstrate incorrect form followed by correct form.
5. Demonstrate for clarification.

■ Unison versus Free Practice

The walk-through for a new step should be done in unison responding to teaching cues. The whole motion of the group assists in the learning process and allows the teacher the opportunity to spot problems. Teacher–directed unison practice should be abandoned as soon as a majority have learned the step. Free practice transposes the class into a "natural" situation, more akin to the way it is to be done as a leisure pursuit.

At every level of progress in the teaching and learning process, the student should be made aware of the importance of rhythm and the use of space when moving around the dance floor. Understanding rhythm means that the lead can more creatively combine and lead a variety of dance patterns to any given piece of music. Understanding space means that the lead can lead his partner around the dance floor in the traditional line of direction and at the same time employ steps and dance positions that allow him to steer his partner through and around other dancers without interrupting his or their movements.

■ Dance Lesson Preparation

Teacher preparation should begin with selecting the basic step to be taught. Next analyze the underlying rhythm and know where the accent is placed in the music. Study the style of the movement used in the step and practice with the music so that it can be accurately demonstrated. One teacher will need to know both the lead's and the follow's parts and be able to demonstrate them with a student from time to time. Two teachers demonstrating is a more ideal situation, but one well–prepared teacher can lead a good student after a class walk–through usually without out–of–class practice. In addition, the teacher should carefully analyze the position, leads, style, and teaching cues for both the lead's and follow's parts and develop routines for practicing the step forward, backward, or in place.

■ Sample Lesson Plan

The daily lesson plan should include learning objective, music selection, background information about the dance, teaching progression, and evaluation. Objectives are the perceived outcomes of the lesson. Example: Dance the magic step in time with the music. Choose several musical selections with moderate tempo to provide sameness of beat, yet variety of sound for class practice. Most dances have backgrounds stemming from a country, region, type of music, or a personality. This is a typical and viable model for creating a good and effective lesson plan.

■ Teaching Progression

The teaching progression is the blueprint of the lesson and should be a supportive guide for the teacher and an effective road map for the students to achieve the objectives of the plan. The lesson should proceed from the known to the unknown. Begin the lesson with a warm–up and review, which means dancing and polishing something already learned. Follow with new material that should constitute the greater portion of the lesson. Then add free practice time and give individual assistance as needed. Throughout the lesson be alert to partner changes so that there is an ample exchange of opportunities for each student to dance with skilled and less skilled dancers. The evaluation should guide the teacher to class needs and provide students with some positive sense of their progress. The most important thing is to teach with enthusiasm and make each lesson a fun–filled occasion.

■ Technology Aids Teaching

Modern audio products such as the variable speed tape deck and CD player, wireless microphone systems, and "Dick Tracy–like" wireless remote wristwatch combine to free dance teachers from the stationary microphone and record player. The wireless microphone system consists of a light wire frame attached to the head and plugged into a belt pack transmitter thus giving the teacher complete mobility and easy vocal command during instruction. Depending on the manufacturer, the equipment has a range of 300 to 1000-plus feet and battery life of 15 to 18 hours. The wireless remote wristwatch makes it possible to control one CD and two tape decks. In addition, it starts and stops the music, adjusts the tempo, rewinds, moves fast forward, and can choose tracks on one or two CD decks.

STYLE OF SOCIAL DANCE

Social style ballroom dancing does not follow the rules of competition or dancesport. American Ballroom Dancing has borrowed steps and dances from many, many countries. Few of these are now done in the authentic style of any country. In most cases, it was the rhythmic quality that was fascinating and not its meaning. Therefore, only a semblance of the original style remains in the Latin American dances done on our dance floors.

Particular consideration needs to be given to the importance of the individual as a person and the development of one's own style. Since all individuals are different, it is folly to try to get them all to perform exactly alike. The individual who likes to dance will work for the right feeling and take a pride in the way it looks. The dance will gradually reflect an easy confidence and become part of the individual's personality.

At the beginning, few students realize the importance of good basic posture and footwork to the beauty and style of any dance. An easy, upright, balanced posture and motion of the feet in line with the body will make the dancer look good regardless of how limited the knowledge of steps. *Style* means the specific way of moving in any one dance as influenced by rhythmic qualities of the music, cultural characteristics of a country, or the current style of the movement. Styles of dances change from time to time with the rising popularity of a new star, a new band sound, or a new promotional venture by the popular dance studios.

■ *Levels*

The three main levels of dance steps that are often referred to in ballroom dancing are bronze (beginning), silver (intermediate), and gold (advanced). In relationship to the fox trot and waltz, bronze steps tend to finish with the feet together, whereas silver steps are more progressive, constantly traveling in line of direction.

■ *Footwork in Social Dance*

Footwork is a term used to discuss the manner of using the feet in the performance of dance steps. With the exception of body posture, it has the most significant bearing on form and style. Far too often the placement of the feet and the action of the legs give a distorted appearance to the dance. The beauty, continuity, and balance of a figure may be lost entirely due to any comic and, at the same time, tragic caricature unintentionally given to the motion.

Some general principles are involved in the application of good footwork to good dance style.

1. The weight should be carried on the ball of the foot for easy balance, alert transfer of weight from step to step, and change of direction.
2. The feet should be pointing straight ahead. When moving from one step to another, they should reach straight forward or backward in the direction of the desired action and in line with or parallel to the partner's feet.
3. Any action will start with feet together. When moving, feet should pass as closely as possible. With a few exceptions, the feet should always come together before reaching in a new direction. This is known as a follow-through with the feet, and it is used in the Foxtrot, Waltz, and Tango.

4. The feet are never dragged along the floor from one step to another. There is a light connection to the floor as the foot is moved noiselessly into the next position. Occasionally, as in the Tango, the foot glides smoothly into place and without a scraping sound on the floor.

5. The legs should reach forward or backward from the hip. The action is initiated by stabilizing the trunk and swinging the leg freely.

6. The faster the rhythm, the shorter the step. The slower the rhythm, the more reaching the step.

7. Changes of direction are more readily in balance and under control if initiated when the feet are close together rather than when they are apart.

8. For the specific actions of reaching with one foot forward or backward, as in a corté or a hesitation step, the arch of the foot should be extended and the toe pointed.

9. Turning and pivoting figures are most effectively executed from a small base of support with the action of the lead's and the follow's feet dovetailing nicely. This is possible when the action of the foot is a smooth turn on the ball of the foot with the body weight up, not pressing into the floor.

10. In accordance with the characteristic cultural style of a dance, the footwork will involve specific and stylized placement of the feet. This styling is described with each dance.

■ *One-Step/Dance Walk*

All smooth dances used to have a gliding motion with the ball of the foot. However, change in style now dictated a *dance walk* that is much like a regular walk when moving forward. It is a step forward on the heel of the foot, transferring the weight to the ball of the foot. This action is used by both lead and follow when they are moving forward. The backward step is a long reach to the toe, transferring the weight to the ball of the foot.

In closed dance position, the lead is reaching forward and the follow backward, simultaneously. There is a tendency for the lead to step sideways so as not to step on the follow's foot, but he should step forward directly in line with her foot. The follow consequently must reach backward into her step not only to avoid being stepped on but to give the lead room for his step. Master dance teachers have been quoted as saying, "If the follow gets her toe stepped on, it is her own fault." This reemphasizes the point that the dance walk is a long reaching step and both lead and follow must learn to reach out confidently. It is this reach that makes the style smooth and beautiful and provides contrast to other smaller steps. Taking all small steps gives the style a cramped, insecure feeling. The following points describe the mechanics of the forward dance walk.

1. The body sways forward from the ankles. The weight is on the ball of the foot.

2. The trunk is stabilized firmly. The leg swings forward from the hip joint. The reach results in a long step rather than a short, choppy step. An exaggerated knee bend will cause bobbing up and down.

3. The foot swings forward and the heel is placed on the floor first, followed by a transfer of weight to the ball of the foot. The feet never drag along the floor.

4. The legs are kept close together, with the feet passing closely together. The toes are facing straight ahead.

5. The lead and the follow dance on the same forward line. One should avoid letting one's feet straddle the partner's feet.

The backward dance walk is not an easy movement because one feels unstable moving backward. It should be practiced particularly by the follow since she will be moving backward a large part of the time.

1. The body weight is over the ball of the foot. Be careful not to lean forward or backward. The follow is pressing against the lead's hand at her back.

2. The trunk is stabilized firmly. The leg swing backward from the hip joint with a long, smooth reach. Avoid unnecessary knee bend of the standing leg.

3. The foot is placed backward on the toe with weight transferring to the ball of the foot. The weight remains on the ball of the foot, the heel coming down only momentarily during the next step.

4. The legs and feet pass as closely as possible and in a straight line. Avoid toeing out, heeling out, and swinging backward outside of the straight line.

DANCE POSITIONS

Successful performance with a dance partner depends on learning how to assume the dance positions* most often used in social dance: *closed position, open* or *conversation position, left parallel position, swing out* or *flirtation position, side car, shine, wrap, reverse open,* and *side-by-side position*. Dancers should learn how to assume the closed position as soon as they begin working with a partner. The results will lead to good balance, comfort, and confidence in leading and security in following. The closed position is the basic dance position. The others are adaptations of it.

■ *Closed Position*

Each factor in the analysis of the closed position is significant. It is not a mere formality. Those who are learning dance will tend to form better dance habits if they understand specifically how the position aids the dance rather than being left to manage as best they can.

1. **Partners should stand facing each other, slightly offset to their left, with shoulders parallel.** The right foot of each partner should be placed between the partner's feet, near the front of the foot. When bending knees they should not knock together. A comfortable distance should be maintained. The body posture is in good alignment.

2. **The feet should be together and pointing straight ahead.** The weight is over the balls of the feet.

3. **The lead's right arm** is placed around the follow so that his arm **gives her security and support. The right hand is placed in the center of the follow's back, just below the shoulder blades.** The lead should keep his right elbow lifted to help support the follow's left arm. The fingers should be closed and the hand almost flat so that the lead can lead with the fingers or the heel of the hand. The lead's arm is extended away from his body with the elbow pointing slightly out to the right side. The lead's left hand should be no higher than the shortest person's shoulder level. A majority of leads are initiated by the lead's shoulders, right arm, and hand.

4. **The follow's left arm rests gently but definitely in contact with the lead's upper arm** and the hand should lie along the back of the lead's shoulder as is comfortable. The follow's ability to follow is often determined by her response to the action of the lead's arm.

5. **The follow should arch her back against the lead's right hand and move with it.** All pressure leads for change of step will come from the lead's right hand, and she will feel them instantly.

---

* Refer to the Glossary for descriptions of other positions.

DANCE POSITIONS*

1. Back Cross

2. Butterfly

3. Challenge
   Shine

4. Cross

5. Closed

6. Conversation
   Open

7. Cuddle

8. Escort

9. Face Off

10. Hammerlock

*Detailed description for each position is given in the Glossary.

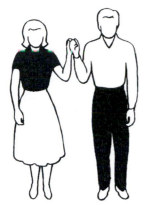

11. Inside Hands Joined.
    Side by Side. Couple

12. Jockey

13. Latin Social

14. Left Parallel.
    Side Car

15. Little Window

16. Octopus

17. Promenade,
    Ballroom

18. Pigeon Wing
    Right Hand Start

19. Country
    Western

20. Reverse Open

21. Reverse Varsouvienne

22. Right Parallel.
(Outside position)

23. Semiopen

24. Shoulder-Waist

25. Social Swing

26a. Swing Out.
Flirtation

26b. Swing Out–
Lindy Style

27. Two Hands Joined.
Facing

28. Varsouvienne
(Traditional)
Sweetheart
(Modern)

29. Yoke, Bridge

6. **The follow's free hand is raised sideways and the lead holds the follow's right hand in his left hand approximately between them at a level just above the follow's shoulder.** The lead may let her fingers rest on his upturned palm, or he may grasp lightly with his thumb against her fingers and close his fingers around the back of her hand. He should not push with his hand.

7. **Both the lead and follow should look at each other or over the partner's right shoulder.**

8. **Tone is essential.** A limp body or a limp hand is the surest indication of insecurity; a poor lead elicits a slow response. Dancers need to understand the difference between tension, which does not allow for easy moving along with one's partner, and relaxation, which cannot respond readily to change. An in-between state of body alertness—called *resistance*—is more desirable.

Some **common errors** in the use of closed position are the following:

1. Partner standing at an angle in a half-open position. This causes diagonal motion of the footwork and is uncomfortable.

2. Partner too far away.

3. Lack of support in the lead's right arm.

4. Lack of contact of the follow's left arm.

5. Primary use of lead's left hand to lead by a pushing or pumping action.

6. Lack of resistance by either lead or follow.

7. Lead's right hand too high on follow's back, pulling her off balance.

8. Follow's weight back on heels.

9. Lead leaning forward from the waist so is off balance.

10. Lead pulling back with his left shoulder and hand, causing an awkward angle of motion.

11. Follow leaning heavily on partner's arm.

■ Trends in Vocabulary and Leading

The closed dance position is presently being referred to as the *frame*. The term conjures a body position of substance, firmness, or presence as opposed to "limp" or "just there." In addition, the terms "man and lady" or "man and woman" are being replaced by "lead" and "follow." In some cases, the traditional "women follow–men lead" notion is being reversed. The reversal is used to stimulate sensitivity to a partner's responsibilities. Switching roles, albeit temporarily should improve a dancer's ability to lead or to follow.

■ Techniques of Leading and Following

Leading is done primarily by the use of the body, arms, and hands. The lead sets the rhythm, decides what steps are to be used, and controls the direction and progression around the floor. The follow is completely dependent upon her partner. Therefore, an alert yet easy posture should be assumed to allow dancers to move as a unit. The firmness of the lead's hand on the follow's back is an important pressure lead for changes in dance position and direction. Through the use of gentle yet firm leads, the lead can make dancing a mutually pleasant experience.

The follow's responsibility is to follow her partner and adapt to any rhythm or style. She should maintain an easy resistance to give the lead an alert, movable partner to lead. The follow should always maintain contact with her partner's upper right arm and shoulder and give firm resistance to his hand on her back. Should the lead be a poor leader, the follow must then pay close attention to his body movement, particularly the shoulders and chest, in order to follow. When in a position apart from a partner, following requires a firm controlled arm that responds to a lead by simultaneous action of the body. In the challenge position, the follow's only lead is visual. She must be alert and follow her partner's action by watching him. Some general rules for following are: (a) keep the lead's rhythm and be alert to his leads; (b) support one's own weight; (c) step straight back with a reaching motion to give partner room to step straight ahead; (d) pass feet close together; (e) know the basic steps and leads; (f) try not to anticipate partner's action; and (g) work on maintaining proper body alignment and good easy posture.

SPECIFIC DIRECTIONS FOR LEADING

1. **To lead the first step,** the lead should precede the step off with the left foot by an upbeat, forward motion of the body.

2. **To lead a forward moving pattern,** the lead should give a forward motion in the body, including the right arm, which will direct the follow firmly in the desired direction.

3. **To lead a backward moving pattern,** the lead should use pressure of the right hand. This will draw the follow forward in the desired direction.

4. **To lead a sideward moving pattern in closed position,** the lead should use pressure of the right hand to the left or right to indicate the desired direction.

5. **To lead a box step,** the lead should use a forward body action followed by right–hand pressure and right–elbow pull to the right to take the follow into the forward sequence of the box. Forward pressure of the right hand followed by pressure to the left side takes her into the back sequence of the box.

6. **To lead a box turn,** with slight pressure of the right hand, the lead should use the right arm and shoulder to guide or bank her into the turn. The shoulders press forward during the forward step and draw backward during the backward step.

7. **To lead into an open position,** or conversation position, the lead should use pressure with the heel of the hand to turn the follow into open position. The right elbow lowers to the side. The lead must simultaneously turn his own body, not just the follow, so that they end facing the same direction. The left arm relaxes slightly and the left hand sometimes gives the lead for steps in open position.

8. **To lead from open to closed position,** the lead should use pressure of the right hand and raise the right arm up to standard position to move the follow into closed position. She should not have to be pushed, but should swing easily into closed position as she feels the arm lifting. She should come clear around to face the lead squarely.

9. **To lead into right parallel position** (left reverse open position), the lead should not use pressure of his right hand, but rather should raise his right arm, rotating her counterclockwise one–eighth of a turn while he rotates counterclockwise one–eighth of a turn. This places the lead and the follow off to the side of each other, facing opposite directions. The follow is to the right of him but slightly in front of him. The lead should avoid turning too far so as to be side by side as this results in poor style and awkward and uncomfortable motion. The lead's left hand may assist the lead by pulling toward his left shoulder.

10. **To lead from right parallel position to left parallel position,** the lead should pull with his right hand, lowering the right arm, and push slightly with his left hand causing a rotation clockwise about a quarter turn until the follow is to the left of him but slightly in front of him. They are not side by side.

11. **To lead a hesitation step,** the lead should use pressure of the right hand on the first step and sudden body tension to control a hold of position as long as desired.

12. **To lead all turns,** the lead dips his shoulder in the direction of the turn, and his upper torso turns before his leg and foot turn.

13. **To lead into a pivot turn,** clockwise, the lead should hold the follow slightly closer, but with sudden body tension. Resistance is exerted outward by both the lead and follow leaning away from each other in order to take advantage of the centrifugal force of the circular motion. The right foot steps between partner's feet, forward on the line of direction, while the left foot reaches across the line of direction and turns on the ball of the foot about three–quarters of the way around.

14. **To lead into a corté** (dip) the lead should use firm pressure of the right hand with sudden increased body tension going into the preparation step. Then the lead should draw his partner forward toward him as he steps back into the dip. The left foot taking the dip backward should carry the weight, and careful balance of the weight should remain over that foot. Pressure is released as they recover to the other foot.

15. **Finger pressure leads and arm control** are important. Many times the lead's only contact with his partner is with one hand or changing from hand to hand. A soft, gentle hand hold and a limp arm make it impossible to lead the variations of Swing, Cha Cha Cha, or Rumba. It is necessary that the follow exert slight resistance to the lead's grasp so that pressure in any direction is reacted to instantly. Both the lead and follow should maintain elbow control by holding the arm firmly in front of the body with elbows down and always slightly bent. The arm is seldom allowed to extend in the elbow as this destroys the spring action needed to move out and in and under without jerking. The fingers often need to slip around the partner's without actually losing contact, in order to maintain comfortable action of the wrist and arm.

16. **To change the rhythm pattern,** the lead exerts extra pressure with the right hand and pushes a little harder from the chest.

17. **Visual lead.** When partners are apart, as in the shine position of Cha Cha Cha, the follow watches her partner closely.

■ Following

The follow's responsibility in dancing is to follow her partner and adapt to any rhythm or style he dances. She should maintain an easy resistance, not rigidity or tension, throughout the body. This is referred to as having *tone*. If there is no tone and the follow is too relaxed or stiff, leading becomes very difficult. The lead's ability to lead his partner will be enhanced when she has tone. In other words, it takes cooperation for two people to dance well, the same way it takes two people for a satisfactory hand–shake. The follow should always maintain contact with her partner's upper right arm and shoulder and give resistance against his hand at her back, moving with it as it guides her. If the lead is a poor leader, then the follow must pay close attention to his body movement, particularly his chest and shoulder movement, in order to follow. Following, when in an apart position, requires a firm, controlled arm that responds to a lead by simultaneous action of the body. A limp arm with no resultant body response makes leading difficult in Swing, Rumba, and Cha Cha Cha. In the challenge position, the follow's only lead is visual. She must be alert and follow her partner's action by watching him. The good dancer will aim to dance with beauty of form. The follow can make a poor dancer look good or a good dancer look excellent. She can also cramp his style if she takes too small a step, has poor control of balance, dances with her feet apart, dances at an awkward angle, or leans forward.

GENERAL RULES FOR FOLLOWING

1. Keep the lead's rhythm.
2. Be alert to partner's lead.
3. Support one's own weight. Arch the back and move with the partner's hand.
4. Step straight backward with reaching motion so as to give the partner room to step straight ahead.
5. Pass the feet close together.
6. Know the basic steps and basic leads.
7. Try not to anticipate partner's action, just move with it.
8. Give careful thought to proper body alignment and good posture.

RHYTHM AND METER

■ Rhythm

Rhythm is the regular pattern of movement and/or sound. It is a relationship between time and force factors. It is felt, seen, or heard.

■ Beat

Beat is the basic unit that measures time. The duration of time becomes established by the beat, or the pulse, as it is repeated. It is referred to as the *underlying beat*.

■ Accent

Accent is the stress placed on a beat to make it stronger or louder than the others. The primary accent is on the first beat of the music. There may be a secondary accent.

When the accent is placed on the unnatural beat (the off beat), the rhythm is *syncopated*.

■ Measure

A *measure* is one group of beats made by the regular occurrence of the heavy accent. It represents the underlying beat enclosed between two adjacent bars on a musical staff.

■ Meter

Meter is the metric division of a measure into parts of equal time value and regular accents. Meter can be recognized by listening for the accent on the first beat.

■ Time Signature

Time signature is a symbol (e.g., 2/4) that establishes the duration of time. The upper number indicates the number of beats per measure, and the lower number indicates the note value that receives one beat.

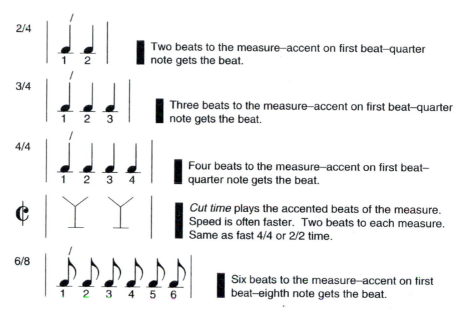

2/4 — Two beats to the measure—accent on first beat—quarter note gets the beat.

3/4 — Three beats to the measure—accent on first beat—quarter note gets the beat.

4/4 — Four beats to the measure—accent on first beat—quarter note gets the beat.

¢ — *Cut time* plays the accented beats of the measure. Speed is often faster. Two beats to each measure. Same as fast 4/4 or 2/2 time.

6/8 — Six beats to the measure—accent on first beat—eighth note gets the beat.

■ Note Values

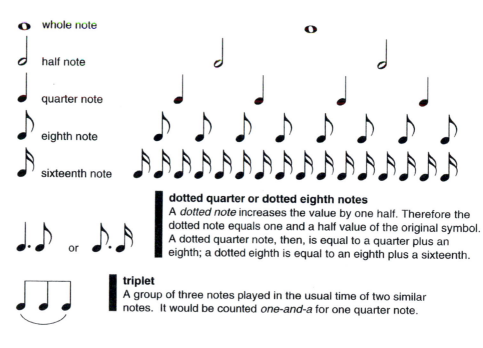

whole note

half note

quarter note

eighth note

sixteenth note

dotted quarter or dotted eighth notes
A *dotted note* increases the value by one half. Therefore the dotted note equals one and a half value of the original symbol. A dotted quarter note, then, is equal to a quarter plus an eighth; a dotted eighth is equal to an eighth plus a sixteenth.

triplet
A group of three notes played in the usual time of two similar notes. It would be counted *one-and-a* for one quarter note.

■ Line Values

Whereas the musical notation establishes the *relative value of beats*, these same relative values can be represented by lines:

one whole note	————————————————————
two half notes	——————————— ———————————
four quarter notes	————— ————— ————— —————
eight eighth notes	— — — — — — — —
sixteen sixteenth notes	– – – – – – – – – – – – – – – –

■ Phrase

A musical sentence, or *phrase*, can be felt by listening for a complete thought. This can be a group of measures, generally four or eight measures. A group of phrases can express a group of complete thoughts that are related just as a group of sentences expresses a group of complete thoughts in a paragraph. Groups of phrases are generally 16 or 32 measures long.

■ Tempo

Tempo is the rate of speed at which music is played. Tempo influences the mood or the quality of music and movement. Sometimes at the beginning of the music or the dance, the tempo is established by a metronome reading. For example, metronome 128 means the equal recurrence of beats at the rate of 128 per minute.

■ Rhythm Pattern

The *rhythm pattern* is the grouping of beats that repeat for the pattern of a dance step, just as for the melody of a song. The rhythm pattern must correspond to the underlying beat. Example: meter or underlying beat 4/4.

rhythm pattern
underlying beat

■ Even Rhythm

When the beats in the rhythm pattern are all the same value (note or line value)—all long (slow) or all short (quick)—the rhythm is *even*. Examples: walk, run, hop, jump, leap, Waltz, Schottische.

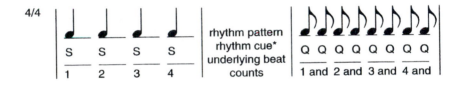

rhythm pattern
rhythm cue*
underlying beat
counts

*S = Slow; Q = Quick

■ *Uneven Rhythm*

When the beats in the rhythm pattern are not all the same value, but are any combination of slow and quick beats, the rhythm is *uneven.* Examples: Two–Step, Foxtrot.

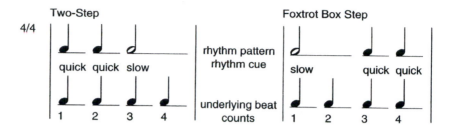

A *dotted beat* borrows half the value of itself again. Examples: skip, slide, gallop.

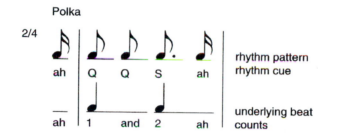

When the note comes before the bar, it is called a *pick-up beat.*

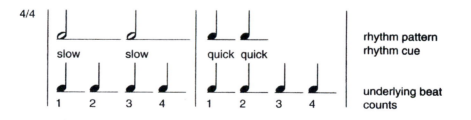

■ *Broken Rhythm*

Broken rhythm is a combination of slow and quick beats when the rhythm pattern takes more than one measure. A repetition begins in the middle of the measure. Example: Magic Step in the Foxtrot.

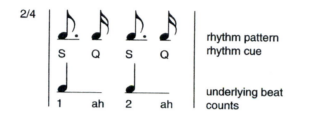

ANALYSIS OF A BASIC RHYTHM

A teacher should thoroughly understand the complete analysis of each basic dance step to be taught. The following example shows the eight related parts of an analysis. Each basic dance step has been analyzed in this manner (including the basic steps of Social Dance below).

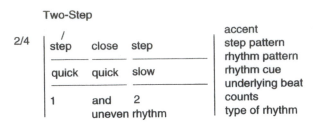

Two-Step

2/4	/ step	close	step		accent step pattern rhythm pattern
	quick	quick	slow		rhythm cue underlying beat
	1	and uneven rhythm	2		counts type of rhythm

BASIC DANCE STEPS

■ *Shuffle, Dance Walk, or Glide*

1. An easy, light step, from one foot to the other, in even rhythm.
2. Different from a walk in that the weight is over the ball of the foot.
3. The feet remain lightly in contact with the floor.

■ *Two-Step*

1. 2/4 or 4/4 meter.
2. Uneven rhythm.
3. Step forward on left foot, close right to left, take weight on right, step left again. Repeat, beginning with right.
4. The rhythm is quick, quick, slow.

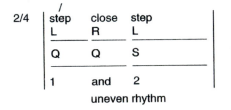

2/4	/ step L	close R	step L
	Q	Q	S
	1	and	2
		uneven rhythm	

■ *Waltz*

1. 3/4 meter—accent first beat.
2. A smooth, graceful dance step in even rhythm.
3. Ladder step consists of three steps; step forward on the left, step to the side with the right, close left to right, take weight on left.

3/4	/ fwd L	side R	close L	fwd R	side L	close R
	S	S	S	S	S	S
	1	2	3	1	2	3
			even rhythm			

4. The **Box Waltz** is the basic pattern for the Box Waltz turn. Step left forward, step right sideward, passing close to the left foot, close left to right, taking weight left; step right backward, step left sideward, passing close to the right foot, close right to left, take weight right. *Cue:* Forward side close, back side close.

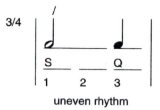

3/4	fwd	side	close	back	side	close
	L	R	L	R	L	R
	S	S	S	S	S	S
	1	2	3	1	2	3

even rhythm

5. The **Running Waltz** used so often in European Folk Dances is a tiny three–beat running step with an accent on the first beat, three beats to each measure.

6. **Canter Waltz** rhythm is an uneven rhythm in Waltz time with the action taking place on beats one and three. The rhythm is slow, quick; slow, quick or long, short.

3/4			
	S		Q
	1	2	3

uneven rhythm

BASIC DANCE TURNS

Using the fundamental dance steps, partners may turn clockwise or counterclockwise. Basically, if the lead is leading with the left, the turn is counterclockwise; if he is lead–ing with the right, the turn is clockwise. But in Folk Dance, the majority of the partner turns are clockwise. A successful turn actually starts with the preceding step, the lead's back to center and his body moving into the turn. The lead steps left backward in the line of direction, which allows his right foot to lead on the second step.

■ *Two-Step Turn Clockwise*

The Two–Step rhythm is uneven 2/4 or 4/4 meter with a quick–quick–slow pattern. There is a half–turn on each measure (2/4 meter). The starting position is closed, with the lead's back to center of the circle. *The turn is on the second count.*

LEFT-FOOT SEQUENCE (LEAD):

Count 1   Step left sideward.

Count and   Close right to left, taking weight on right.

Count 2   Step left around partner, toeing in and pivoting clockwise on the ball of the foot a half–turn around.

RIGHT-FOOT SEQUENCE (FOLLOW):

Count 1   Step right sideward.

Count and   Close left to right, taking weight on left.

Count 2   Step right forward between partner's feet and pivoting clockwise on the ball of the foot a half–turn around.

NOTE: The lead starts with the left sequence, the follow starts with the right sequence. After a half–turn, the follow then starts with the left sequence and the lead with the right sequence. They continue to alternate. By this process of *dovetailing with the feet*, lead and follow can turn easily without stepping on each other's feet. Couple progresses in the line of direction as they turn.

STYLE: The steps should be small and close to partner. The body leans back and aids in the turn. The turn is on the ball of the foot. Each partner must give the impetus for the turn by pivoting on his or her own foot.

LEAD: Closed position, the lead should have a firm right hand on the small of the follow's back so that she can lean back against it. His right arm guides her as he turns.

CUES:

1. *Left-Foot Sequence:* side close around.
   Right-Foot Sequence: side close between.

2. Practicing together in closed position.
   Side close turn, side close turn.

■ *Waltz Turn*

The Waltz rhythm is even 3/4 meter. Three patterns are presented: the Box Waltz, traditional step–side–close, and Running Waltz pattern.

BOX WALTZ TURN—CLOCKWISE, COUNTERCLOCKWISE

The Box Waltz turn is used in social dancing and in some American Folk Dances and can go either to the left in a counterclockwise turn or to the right in a clockwise turn, depending on which foot leads the turn.

CLOCKWISE TURN

The clockwise turn is the turn most often used for Folk Dances. Two patterns are presented, the first based on the traditional step–side–close pattern and the second on the running Waltz pattern. It is in 3/4 meter.

STEP-SIDE-CLOSE PATTERN (TRADITIONAL)

LEFT-FOOT SEQUENCE (LEAD):

Step left around partner, pivoting on the ball of the foot a half–turn clockwise (count 1). Step right sideward in line of direction (count 2). Close left to right, take weight left (count 3).

RIGHT-FOOT SEQUENCE (FOLLOW):

Step right forward between partner's feet, pivoting on the ball of the foot a half–turn clockwise (count 1). Step left sideward in the line of direction (count 2). Close right to left, take weight right (count 3).

NOTE: The lead starts with the left sequence, the follow with the right sequence. After a half–turn, the follow starts with the left sequence and the lead with the right sequence. They continue to alternate. By this process of dovetailing the feet, dancers can turn easily without stepping on each other's feet.

STYLE: The steps are small and close to partner. The pivot halfway around is on the ball of the foot on the first count. Each partner is responsible for supplying the impetus for the ball of the foot turn.

LEAD: The lead has a firm right hand at the follow's back. She leans back and is guided into the turn by his firm right hand and arm.

CUES:

1. *Left-Foot Sequence:* around side close.
   Right-Foot Sequence: between side close.
2. Practice together in closed position.
   Turn side close, turn side close.

STEP-STEP-CLOSE PATTERN

LEFT-FOOT SEQUENCE (LEAD):

Step left in the line of direction (toeing in, heel leads), pivoting on the ball of the foot and starting a half–turn clockwise (count 1). Take two small steps, right, left, close to first step, completing half–turn (counts 2 and 3).

RIGHT-FOOT SEQUENCE (FOLLOW):

Step right in line of direction (toeing out) *between partner's feet,* pivoting on the ball of the foot, starting a half–turn clockwise (count 1). Take two small steps, left, right, close to first step, completing half–turn (counts 2 and 3).

NOTE:

1. When the lead steps backward left, the right foot leads the clockwise turn.
2. The lead starts with the left sequence, the follow with the right sequence. After a half–turn, the follow starts with the left sequence and the lead with the right sequence. They continue to alternate. When doing left-foot sequence, step backward in line of direction; when doing the right–foot sequence, step forward (but not as long a step as the first step in the other sequence). The dancers are turning on each count, but steps on counts 2 and 3 are almost in place. *Both feet are together on count 3.*

LEAD: The Lead has a firm right hand at the follow's back. She leans back and is guided into the turn by his firm right hand and arm.

CUES:

Left-Foot Sequence: Back turn turn.
Right-Foot Sequence: Forward turn turn.

REVERSE DIRECTION OF TURN

If turning counterclockwise, the left foot leads. If turning clockwise, the right foot leads. To change leads from left to right or right to left, one measure (3 beats) is needed for transition. A balance step backward or one Waltz step forward facilitates the transition. Or turning counterclockwise, after a left Waltz step, immedi–ately reverse direction with a right Waltz step, turning clockwise (a more difficult maneuver). Eventually the lead comes back to a left one, and another transition occurs.

2

BALLROOM FAVORITES

Foxtrot

THE *FOXTROT*, AS A present–day form, is of relatively recent origin. The only truly American form of Ballroom Dance, it has had many steps and variations through the years. The Foxtrot gets its name from a musical comedy star, Henry Fox, of the years 1913–1914 (Hostetler 1952), who danced a fast but simple trotting step to ragtime music in one of the Ziegfeld shows of that time. As an additional publicity stunt, the theater management requested that a star nightclub performer, Oscar Duryea, introduce the step to the public but found that it had to be modified somewhat, because a continuous trotting step could not be maintained for long periods without exhausting effort. Duryea simplified the step so that it became four walking steps alternating with eight quick running steps. This was the first Foxtrot.

Since that time, under the influence of Vernon and Irene Castle and a series of pro–fessional dancers, the Foxtrot has been through a gradual refining process and has developed into a beautifully smooth dance. It claims considerable popularity today.

Music from ragtime through the blues on down to modern jazz and swing has had its effect on the Foxtrot. The original Foxtrot was danced to a lively 2/4 rhythm. Its two parent forms were the One–Step, 2/4 –––– quick quick quick quick rhythm; the other was the Two–Step, 2/4 |–––|–––| quick quick slow or step–close–step. Both of these forms are danced today but have given way to a slower, smoother 4/4 time and a more streamlined style. The Foxtrot is danced in three tempos (slow, medium, and fast) and can be adapted to almost any tempo played in the music.

The basic Foxtrot steps can be used together in any combination or sequence. A dancer who knows the basic steps and understands the fundamentals of rhythm can make up his or her own combinations easily and gradually develop the possibilities for variation in position, direction, and tempo.

FOXTROT RHYTHM

The modern Foxtrot in 4/4 time, or cut time, has four quarter beats or their equivalent to each measure. Each beat is given the same amount of time, but there is an accent on the first and third beats of the measure. When a step is taken on each beat (1–2–3–4), these are called *quick beats*. When steps are taken only on the two accented beats (1 and 3), they are twice as long and are called *slow beats*.

4/4 | — — — — |
| Q Q Q Q | One-Step
| 1 2 3 4 |

4/4 | ——— ——— |
| S S | Dance walk
| 1–2 3–4 |

A use of these quick and slow beats and a combination of them into rhythm patterns form the basis for all of the modern Foxtrot steps. There are two patterns used predominantly: the magic step and the Westchester box step.

■ *Magic Step*

The magic step pattern represents broken rhythm as it takes a measure and half of music and may be repeated from the middle of the measure. It is an uneven rhythm pattern, slow slow quick quick.

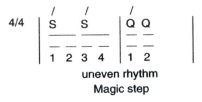

uneven rhythm
Magic step

■ *Westchester Box Step*

The Westchester box step is a one-measure pattern, but it takes two measures to complete the box. The rhythm is uneven, slow quick quick. The rhythm may also be played in cut time, but it is still slow quick quick. Beats 1 and 2 are put together to make 1 beat. Beats 3 and 4 are put together to make 1 beat. The time signature for cut time is ¢. It is played faster and feels very much like 2/4 time.

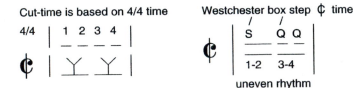

FOXTROT STYLE

Foxtrot style truly reflects its American origin. It is the least affected of any of the Ballroom Dances. Completely without stylized or eccentric arm, foot, head, or torso movement, the Foxtrot is a beautifully smooth dance. The body is held easily erect and follows the foot pattern in a relaxed way with little up and down or sideward movement. The good dancer glides normally along the floor and blends the various steps together without bobbing or jerking. This effect is accomplished by long, reaching steps with only as much knee bend as is needed to transfer the weight smoothly from step to step. It gives the Foxtrot a streamlined motion and a simple beauty of form that can be enjoyed without strain or fatigue, dance after dance. As one becomes more and more skillful at putting together steps for the Foxtrot, there will be increasing joy derived from the tremendous variety of quick and slow combinations.

■ *Magic Step Series*

Magic Step (Basic Step)	Promenade with an Arch	The Conversation Pivot
Open Magic Step (Promenade)	Rock, Recover	The Corté
Magic Left Turn	Right and Left Parallel	

The magic step series was created by Arthur Murray (1954). It is called by this name because it can be varied in a surprising number of ways. The pattern is uneven rhythm and requires a measure and a half for one basic step. This is called broken rhythm.

MAGIC STEP (BASIC STEP)

(Closed position)

STEPS	4/4 COUNTS	RHYTHM CUE
Step L forward	1–2	slow
Step R forward	3–4	slow
Step L sideward, a short step	1	quick
Close R to L, take weight on R	2	quick

STEP CUE:

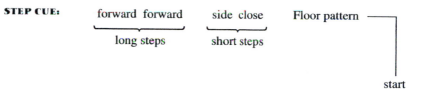

STYLE: The forward steps should be long, smooth, walking steps, straight ahead. The woman, moving backward, takes a long step reaching from hip to toe.

LEAD: A body and right arm lead forward.

VARIATIONS: The following three techniques are used for maneuvering in a closed dance position.

1. Forward or backward—the lead may maneuver forward or backward if he is aware of the traffic around him. The lead to move backward is a pressure lead at the follow's back during the quick quick beats and then a step into the backward direction on the next slow beat. Generally the lead will not have room to move backward more than one or two consecutive patterns.

2. Right or left—the lead may maneuver to the right or to the left to go around another couple. He will change direction on the quick quick beats by use of a pressure lead with his right hand and turn his body at the same time one–eighth of a turn to the right so as to travel diagonally outward or one–eighth turn to the left so as to travel diagonally inward beginning with the next slow beat. The right turn is particularly handy in leading a partner out of a crowded situation away from the center of the floor. Closed position is retained throughout.

3. Dance in place—used on a crowded dance floor. Closed dance position:

STEPS	4/4 COUNTS	RHYTHM CUE
Step sideward L, slide R to L, no weight change	1–2	slow
Step sideward R, slide L to R, no weight change	3–4	slow
Step sideward L	1	quick
Close R to L, take weight R	2	quick

STEP CUE: Step slide, step slide, quick quick.

STYLE: The steps are very small.

LEAD: Increase pressure with the right hand to keep the follow from stepping back. Indicate sideward action.

NOTE: The lead may maneuver this in–place pattern into a turn counterclockwise by the use of the right hand and elbow.

OPEN MAGIC STEP (PROMENADE)

(Closed position)

STEPS	4/4 COUNTS	RHYTHM CUE
Step L forward	1–2	slow
Step R forward	3–4	slow
Step L forward a short step, turning to open dance position	1	quick
Close R to L, take weight R	2	quick
Step L forward in open position	3–4	slow
Step R forward	1–2	slow
Step L forward a short step	3	quick
Close R to L, take weight R	4	quick
Step L forward	1–2	slow
Step R forward	3–4	slow
Step L forward a short step, turning to closed position	1	quick
Close R to L, take weight R	2	quick

STEP CUE: Slow slow quick quick.

STYLE: It is a heel lead on the slow beats in open position for both the lead and follow.

LEAD: To lead into an open position or promenade, the lead should use pressure with the heel of the right hand to turn the follow into open position. The right elbow lowers to the side. The lead must simultaneously turn his own body, not just the follow so that they end facing the same direction. The left arm relaxes slightly and the left hand sometimes gives the lead for steps in the open position.

LEAD: To lead from open to closed position the lead should use pressure of the right hand and raise the right arm up to standard position to move the follow into closed position. The follow should not have to be pushed but should swing easily into closed position as she feels the arm lifting. She should move completely around to face the lead squarely.

LEAD: The lead may wish to return to closed position on the quick beats following the first two slows in open position.

NOTE: It is possible to maneuver when going into open position so that the couple opens facing the line of direction and afterward closes with the lead still facing the line of direction, starting from closed position as follows:

MAGIC LEFT TURN

STEPS	4/4 COUNTS	RHYTHM CUE
Step L forward	1–2	slow
Step R forward	3–4	slow
Step L, R moving around the follow on the L side while turning her halfway around to open position	1–2	quick, quick
Step L forward in open position moving in line of direction	3–4	slow
Step R forward	1–2	slow
Step L, R in place, bringing the follow around to face the closed dance position	3–4	quick quick

STEP CUE: Slow slow come around/slow slow in place.

STYLE: The follow must be sure to swing around, facing the lead, into a correct closed dance position while taking two quick beats.

LEAD: The lead must start bringing his right elbow up to indicate to the follow that he is going into closed position on the first quick beat.

NOTE: Any number of open magic steps may be done consecutively when traveling in the line of direction without fear of interfering with the dancing of other couples.

PROMENADE WITH AN ARCH

(Open–promenade position)

Starting in promenade position, the lead arches the following under his arm, ending in closed position.

STEPS	RHYTHM CUE
Lead steps L forward, lifting L arm up	slow
Follow steps R forward	
Lead steps R forward, giving the follow a gentle push on her back,	slow
turning her under the lead's L arm	
Follow steps R forward, pivoting 270° (3/4 turn) to face partner	
Lead steps L forward, turning to close position	quick
Close R to L, take weight R	quick

ROCK, RECOVER

(Closed position)

STEPS	4/4 COUNTS	RHYTHM CUE
Step L forward a short step	1–2	slow
Step R backward, toe in and turn counterclockwise one-quarter	3–4	slow
Step in place L, toeing out L, and turning one-quarter counterclockwise	1	quick
Step R to L, take weight R, and finish the one-half turn	2	quick
Repeat to make a full turn		

STEP CUE: Rock   rock   step   close.
           S   S   Q   Q

STYLE: The slow steps forward and backward are like short rocking steps, but the body is straight, not leaning.

LEAD: The lead must strongly increase pressure at the follow 's back on the first step so that she will not swing her left foot backward. Then he uses his firm right arm to turn her with him counterclockwise. As the follow reacts to these two leads, she will step in between the lead's feet and pivot on her left foot as he guides her around.

NOTE: The pattern may be reduced to a quarter–turn at a time, or it may be increased to make a full turn at a time. This variation provides a means of turning in place or of turning to maneuver into position for another variation or for recovering the original line of direction. Because of this, it is often used to tie together all types of Foxtrot variations.

RIGHT AND LEFT PARALLEL MAGIC STEP

(Closed position)

This is a delightful variation involving right and left parallel position.

STEPS	4/4 COUNTS	RHYTHM CUE
Step forward	1–2	slow
Step R forward	3–4	slow
Step L sideward a short step, turning to R parallel position	1	quick
Close R to L, take weight on R	2	quick
Step forward L, diagonally in R parallel position	3–4	slow
Step forward R	1–2	slow
Step in place L, turning in place one-quarter clockwise into L parallel position	3	quick
Close R to L, take weight on R	4	quick
Step forward L in L parallel position	1–2	slow
Step forward R	3–4	slow
Step in place L, turning to R parallel	1	quick
Close R to L, take weight on R	2	quick
Step L forward in R parallel position	3–4	slow
Step R forward	1–2	slow
Step L in place, turning to closed position	3	quick
Close R to L, take weight on R	4	quick

STEP CUE: Slow slow quick quick.

STYLE: The follow in parallel position must reach back parallel to the lead's forward reach.

LEAD: To lead into right parallel position, the lead should not use pressure of his right hand but rather should raise his right arm, rotating the follow counterclockwise one–eighth of a turn while he rotates counterclockwise one–eighth of a turn. This places the lead and follow off to the side of each other, facing opposite directions. The follow is to the right of the lead but slightly in front of him. The lead should avoid turning too far so as to be side by side as this results in poor style and awkward and uncomfortable motion. The lead's left hand may assist the lead by pulling toward his left shoulder.

LEAD: To lead from right parallel position to left parallel position, the lead should pull with his right hand lowering the right arm and push slightly with his left hand, causing a rotation clockwise about a quarter of a turn until the follow is to the left of him but slightly in front of him. They are not side by side.

NOTE: The couple should move forward in a zigzag pattern, down the floor, changing from one parallel position to the other. The lead must be careful to take the quick beats in place as he is changing position in order to make a smooth transition. A more advanced use of this variation is to make a half–turn clockwise in place on the quick beats as the lead changes from right parallel position to left parallel position such that the lead would then travel backward in the line of direction and the follow forward. A half–turn counterclockwise in place would then turn the couple back to right parallel position. Innumerable combinations of this variation will develop as dancers experiment with changes of direction.

THE CONVERSATION PIVOT

(Open position)

STEPS	4/4 COUNTS	RHYTHM CUE
Step L forward	1–2	slow
Step R forward	3–4	slow
Step L around the follow clockwise going into closed position	1–2	slow
Step R between follow's feet and pivot on the R foot, turning clockwise	3–4	slow
Step L forward a short step, taking open position again	1	quick
Close R to L, taking weight R	2	quick

NOTE: Two extra slow beats have been added for this variation, S S S S Q Q.

STEP CUE: Step step pivot pivot quick quick.

STYLE: Couples must hold the body firmly and press outward to move with the centrifugal force of the motion on the pivot turn. The follow will step forward in between the lead's feet on the third slow beat and then around him with her left foot on the fourth slow beat, followed by a quick quick to balance oneself in place.

LEAD: See lead indication above. The pivot turn is only the third and fourth slow beats. Then the lead will lead into open position and take the quick beats.

NOTE: Following this variation it is usually wise to dance one more magic step in open position before leading into the basic closed position. Note details on pivot turn, pp. 35–37.

THE CORTÉ

(Closed position)

A fascinating dip step in magic step rhythm.

STEPS	4/4 COUNTS	RHYTHM CUE
Step L forward	1–2	slow
Step R forward	3–4	slow
Step L sideward a short step	1	quick
Close R to L, take weight on R	2	quick
Dip L backward	3–4	slow
Transfer weight forward onto R foot	1–2	slow
Step L sideward, a short step	3	quick
Close R to L, take weight R	4	quick

STEP CUE: Slow slow   quick quick   dip   recover quick quick.
                     (preparation   (corté)   (weight forward)
                     beats)

STYLE: *Lead*–The weight is transferred onto the left foot as the lead steps backward into the dip. The left knee is bent, the back is straight, the right toe extends forward. *Follow*–Her weight is transferred onto the right foot as she steps forward into the dip. The right knee is bent and directly over her foot. The back is arched, keeping her straight up and down. The left leg is extended strongly from the hip through the knee of the pointed toe. Her head should be turned left to glance at the extended foot. For additional style details, see Tango, The Corté p. 49.

LEAD: To lead into a pivot turn clockwise, the lead should hold the follow slightly closer, but with sudden body tension. Resistance is exerted outward by both the lead and follow leaning away from each other in order to take advantage of the centrifugal force of the circular motion. The right foot steps between partner's feet, forward on line of direction, while the left foot reaches across the line of direction and turns on the ball of the foot about three-quarters of the way around. The lead must take care not to step too long backward or to dip too low as it is difficult for both lead and follow to recover in good style.

NOTE: The exciting part about the corté is that it may be used as a variation in the dance or it may be used as a finishing step at the end of the music. It is perfectly acceptable to end a beat or two in advance and hold the position to the end of the music. It is also acceptable to corté after the music has finished. There is no pressure to get the corté on the last note of the music.

■ *Box Step Series—Westchester*

Westchester Box Step	Bronze Twinkle	Grapevine Step
Box Turn	Twinkle Step (Cross Over)	

The Westchester box is based on slow quick quick rhythm in 4/4 or cut time. It is a one–measure pattern—but it takes two measures to complete the box—with uneven rhythm in a smooth style. It is a combination of dance walk and side close.

WESTCHESTER BOX STEP

(Closed position)

STEPS	4/4 COUNTS	RHYTHM CUE
Step L forward	1–2	slow
Pass R alongside of L, no weight change; step R sideward	3	quick
Close L to R, take weight on L	4	quick
Step R backward	1–2	slow
Pass L alongside of R, no weight change; step L sideward	3	quick
Close R to L, take weight on R	4	quick

STEP CUE: (a) Forward   side   close.
      S   Q   Q
   (b) Backward   side   close
      long steps   short   steps.

Floor pattern

STYLE: The forward step is a heel step. Both forward and backward steps should be long reaching steps. Dancers must not lose a beat by pausing as they slide alongside the standing foot.

LEAD: To lead a box step the lead should use a forward body action followed by right-hand pressure and right elbow pull to the right to take the follow into the forward sequence of the box. Forward pressure of the right hand followed by pressure to the left side takes the follow into the back sequence of the box.

NOTE: The lead must understand the concept of the forward side close as being the forward sequence of the box and the backward side close as being the back sequence of the box. It is important because this terminology will be used in future patterns and leads.

BOX TURN

(Left) (Closed position)

STEPS	4/4 COUNTS	RHYTHM CUE
Step L forward, toe out; turn one-quarter to L	1–2	slow
Step R sideward	3	quick
Close L to R, take weight on L	4	quick
Step R backward, toe in; turn one-quarter to L	1–2	slow
Step L sideward	3	quick
Close R to L, take weight on R	4	quick
Step L forward, toe out; turn one-quarter to L	1–2	slow
Step R sideward	3	quick
Close L to R, take weight on L	4	quick
Step R backward, toe in; turn one-quarter to L	1–2	slow
Step L sideward	3	quick
Close R to L, take weight on R	4	quick

STEP CUE: Turn side close, turn side close.

STYLE: The follow is taking the reverse of this pattern except that, when the follow steps forward with her left foot, instead of toeing out as described for the lead, she steps forward between lead's feet. This style for the follow greatly facilitates the turn.

LEAD: Refer to lead indications above. A cue for the lead might be bank side close, draw side close.

NOTE: The lead may use this turn to maneuver himself into any direction he may wish to use next.

BRONZE TWINKLE

(Closed position)

This is a simple but pretty step turning to open dance position momentarily on the forward sequence.

STEPS	4/4 COUNTS	RHYTHM CUE
Step L forward	1–2	slow
Step R sideward, turning to open position	3	quick
Close L to R, take weight on L	4	quick
Step R forward in open position	1–2	slow
Step L forward, turning on L foot to face partner in closed position	3	quick
Close R to L, take weight R	4	quick

STEP CUE: Forward side close, cross side close.

STYLE: The lead and follow do not open up to a side to side position but open just enough to step forward on the inside foot, which feels like a crossing step. It should be accented by a long reaching step on the heel but not a dipping knee or body action.

LEAD: To lead into an open position or conversation position, the lead should use pressure with the heel of the right hand to turn the follow into open position. The right elbow lowers to the side. The lead must simultaneously turn his own body, not just the follow, so that they end facing the same direction. The left arm relaxes slightly and the left hand sometimes gives the lead for steps in the open position.

LEAD: To lead from open to closed position, the lead should use pressure of the right hand and raise the right arm up to standard position to move the follow into closed position. She should not have to be pushed but should swing easily into closed position as she feels the arm lifting. She should move completely around to face the lead squarely.

NOTE: It is possible to go into this step when the lead is facing out so that the cross step may travel into the line of direction.

TWINKLE STEP (CROSS OVER)

(Closed position)

This is a slow quick quick rhythm using right and left parallel positions, led from the forward sequence of the box pattern.

STEPS	4/4 COUNTS	RHYTHM CUE
Step L forward	1–2	slow
Step R sideward	3	quick
Close L to R, take weight on L	4	quick
Step R diagonally forward in R parallel position	1–2	slow
Step L sideward, turning from R parallel to L parallel position	3	quick
Close R to L, take weight on R	4	quick
Step L diagonally forward in L parallel position	1–2	slow
Step sideward R, turning from L parallel to R parallel position	3	quick
Close L to R, take weight on L	4	quick
Step R diagonally forward in R parallel position	1–2	slow
Step L sideward turning to closed position	3	quick
Close R to L take weight on R	4	quick

STEP CUE: Slow quick quick.

STYLE: The quick steps are small. Changing from one parallel position to the other is done in a very smooth rolling manner. The follow needs lots of practice alone to learn the back side close pattern because it is on the diagonal backward parallel to the lead.

LEAD: To lead into right parallel position the lead should not use pressure of his right hand, but rather should raise his right arm rotating the follow counterclockwise one–eighth of a turn while he rotates counterclockwise one–eighth of a turn. This places the lead and follow off to the side of each other facing opposite directions. The follow is to the right of the lead but slightly in front of him. The lead should avoid turning too far so as to be side by side as this results in poor style and awkward and uncomfortable motion. The lead's left hand may assist the lead by pulling toward his left shoulder.

LEAD: To lead from right parallel position to left parallel position, the lead should pull with his right hand lowering the right arm and push slightly with his left hand, causing a rotation clockwise about a quarter of a turn until the follow is to the left of him but slightly in front of him. They are not side by side.

NOTE: Progress is a zigzag pattern down the floor. The parallel part of the steps may be repeated as many times as desired before going back to closed position.

GRAPEVINE STEP

(Closed position)

It is a beautiful pattern in slow quick quick time with four quick steps added to make the grapevine design, using parallel position.

STEPS	4/4 COUNTS	RHYTHM CUE
Step L forward	1–2	slow
Step R sideward, turning into R parallel position	3	quick
Close L to R, take weight on L	4	quick
Step R diagonally forward in R parallel position	1	quick
Step L sideward, turning to L parallel position	2	quick
Step R diagonally backward in L parallel position	3	quick
Step L sideward, turning to R parallel position	4	quick
Step R forward in R parallel position	1–2	slow
Step L sideward turning to closed position	3	quick
Close R to L, take weight on R	4	quick

STEP CUE:

slow quick quick	quick quick quick quick	slow quick quick
forward sequence of box	grapevine pattern	transition back to closed position

STYLE: Practice on the grapevine step alone will help dancers get this pattern smoothly and beautifully. Cue lead: forward side back side (R, L, R, L) on the grapevine step. Cue follow: back side forward side (L, R, L, R) on the grapevine step.

LEAD: To lead into right parallel position, the lead should not use pressure of his right hand, but rather should raise his right arm, rotating the follow counterclockwise one-eighth of a turn while he rotates counterclockwise one–eighth of a turn. This places the lead and follow off to the side of each other, facing opposite directions. The follow is to the right of the lead but slightly in front of him. The lead should avoid turning too far so as to be side by side as this results in poor style and awkward and uncomfortable motion. The lead's left hand may assist the lead by pulling toward his left shoulder.

LEAD: To lead from right parallel position to left parallel position, the lead should pull with his right hand lowering the right arm and push slightly with his left hand, causing a rotation clockwise about a quarter of a turn until the follow is to the left of him but slightly in front of him. They are not side by side.

LEAD: The lead is from the forward sequence of the box.

NOTE: The lead should maneuver to face out before he starts this step so that the grapevine step may travel in the line of direction. He may maneuver into this by use of a three–quarter turn or a hesitation step.

■ The Pivot Turn

The continuous pivot turn is a series of steps turning clockwise as many beats as desired. The lead should be careful that he has room to turn, as the pivot turn progresses forward in the line of direction if done properly, and he should not turn so many steps as to make his partner dizzy. The principle involved in the footwork is the dovetailing of the feet, which means that the right foot always steps between partner's feet and the left foot always steps around the outside of partner's feet. The pivot turn described here has two slow beats as a preparation followed by four quick beats turning and comes out of it into the box step.

THE PIVOT TURN

(Closed position)

STEPS	4/4 COUNTS	RHYTHM CUE
Step L forward	1–2	slow
Step R forward, starting to turn the body clockwise increasing the body tension	3–4	slow
Step L, toeing in across the line of direction and rolling clockwise three-quarters of the way around on the ball of the L foot	1	quick
Step R, between partner's feet forward in the line of direction, completing one turn	2	quick
Step L, toeing in and reaching forward but across the line of direction, turning clockwise three-quarters as before	3	quick
Step R, between partner's feet forward in the line of direction, completing the second turn	4	quick
Step L forward in the line of direction, not turning but controlling momentum	1–2	slow
Step R sideward	3	quick
Close L to R, take weight on L	4	quick
Step R backward	1–2	slow
Step L sideward	3	quick
Close R to L, taking weight R	4	quick

STEP CUE: Step ready
        S   S
  turn turn turn turn
  Q   Q   Q   Q
  forward   side close
  S   Q   Q
  back side close
  S Q Q

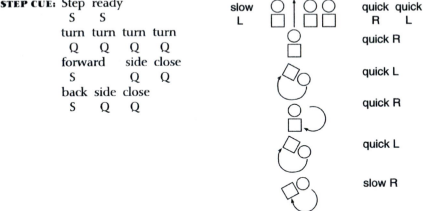

FOLLOW: On the second slow beat, the follow receives the lead as the lead increases body tension. She does the same. Then, on the first quick beat, she has been turned far enough to place her right foot forward in between his feet on the line of direction, left foot across the line of direction, right foot between, left across, and into the box step.

STYLE: They both must lean away, pressing outward like "the water trying to stay in the bucket." The concept of stepping each time in relation to the line of direction is what makes it possible to progress while turning as a true pivot turn should do.

LEAD: To lead all turns, the lead dips his shoulder in the direction of the turn and his upper torso turns before his leg and foot turn.

LEAD: To lead into a pivot turn clockwise, the lead should hold the follow slightly closer, but with sudden body tension. Resistance is exerted outward by both lead and follow leaning away from each other to take advantage of the centrifugal force of the circular motion. The right foot steps between partner's feet, forward on line of direction, while the left foot reaches across the line of direction and turns on the ball of the foot about three–quarters of the way around.

FOXTROT COMBOS

The Foxtrot routines are listed here merely as examples to show how the various steps can be used in combination for practice routines. They are listed from simple to complex. (Closed position unless otherwise indicated.)

1. *Magic Step*
   2 magic steps
   2 open magic steps
   conversation pivot
2. *Magic Step–Box*
   2 magic steps
   1 box step
   2 magic steps (open)
3. *Magic Step/Corté*
   1 magic step (open or closed)
   corté (recover)
   1 side close
   1 box turn
   corté (recover)
4. *Advanced Combo*
   1 magic step
   1 single twinkle to open
   1 single twinkle to left parallel
   1 single twinkle to open
   1 single twinkle to close

Hustle

DISCO BACKGROUND

DISCO STANDS TO THE SEVENTIES as Rock stood to the sixties. *Disco* comes from the word *discotheque*, which in France is a place where records and disques are stored. In the United States, a discotheque is a place where records are played and one can listen or dance to rock music. Disco Dance has become a descriptive term that encompasses a wide variety of dance steps to many musical rhythms. Originally the partners did not touch and the patterns were simple, characterized by (1) stationary base, (2) response to a steady beat–predominantly 4/4 time, (3) action in the upper torso (this is styling of hands and movement of body above the hips), and (4) not following the lead of a partner.

What began as fury and inspiration became fashion. How to keep the momentum going became a major concern as record sales declined and disco attendance dropped. Two events occurred that increased the desire of the whole nation for dance. Studio 54 in New York City proved that a discotheque could work on a grand scale. People wanted an opportunity to exhibit themselves. Gone were the glitter balls; they were replaced by video screens with computer graphics. The disc jockey continued to be in the driver's seat. The dance floor was more spacious. The music and the atmosphere for overstimulation was shared with a profusion of lights, sound, rhythm, and spectacles that could be interpreted as the formula for "pleasure and high times."

The other event was the movie *Saturday Night Fever*. John Travolta strutted and presented a virile young man's need to be assertive, seeking a stage on which to perform.

"Touch dancing" was the new phrase for holding one's partner. The Hustle is credited with bringing people together again on the dance floor. One of the common tunes for dancing was "Feelings"—the dance included body contact, dancing in one spot, responding to the music, and a 4/4 rhythm.

Clubs reopened and new ones arrived to meet the new disco interest. With the Hustle, partners touching once again, the dance studios were back in business. Many of the old forms, like the Lindy and the Latin Dances, and the closed dance position or variations, reappeared.

Hustle with Partner

The partner hustle was popular during the "Disco" dance era (the late '70s). In the mid '90s, the partner hustle resurfaced as part of several "night club" dance styles. Music ranging from 160–190 beats per minute (BPM) may be used.

4/4	rock	step	step		step	
	1	2	3	4	1	2

Directions are for the lead; the follow's part is reversed, except when noted.

BASIC STEP

(Clockwise)

(Two hands joined, lead's hands palm up)

STEPS	4/4 COUNTS	RHYTHM CUE	STEP CUE
Step L backward, a little behind R heel	1	quick	rock
Step R in place	+	quick	step
Step forward L, pivot clockwise 180°	2	slow	step forward
Step back R	3	slow	step back

NOTE: Four basic step equals three measures of music.

STYLE: Keep steps small.

LEAD: The lead pulls down with both hands on count 2, to initiate the partner turn.

STYLE: The forward and back steps are almost in a straight line. The style is very smooth, be careful not to bounce with the "rock step."

SOCIAL BASIC STEP

(Counterclockwise)

Social Swing position with follow at right angle to partner, lead left hand lowered. Lead is pointing left foot to side, follow is pointing right foot forward.

STEPS	4/4 COUNTS	RHYTHM CUE	STEP CUE
Lead's Part			
Step L side	1	quick	side
Step R in place	+	quick	check
Step forward L, crossing in front of right, pivot counter-clockwise 90°	2	slow	cross
Step back R, pivoting counter-clockwise 90°	3	slow	back

NOTE: On count 2, the lead's crossing step is placed in between the follow's feet. He follows her around.

STEPS	4/4 COUNTS	RHYTHM CUE	STEP CUE
Follow's Part			
Step R back, next to left	1	quick	together
Step L forward, pivot counter-clockwise 90°	+	quick	forward
Step R side, pivot counter-clockwise 90°	2	slow	side
Step L back	3	slow	back

THROW OUT

(Social Swing position to Swing Out position)

STEPS	4/4 COUNTS	STEP CUE
Lead's Part		
Step L side	1	side
Step R in place	+	check
Step L forward, crossing in front of right, pivot counterclockwise 90°, releasing follow with R hand	2	cross
Small step R back	3	back
Follow's Part		
Step R back, next to L	1	together
Step L forward	+	forward
Pivot counterclockwise 90° on L, step R side on R	2	side
Pivot counterclockwise 90° on R, step back on L	3	back

STYLE: During this move it is common for both the lead and the follow to point their free arms in the air, similar to John Travolta's famous point pose in *Saturday Night Fever*. At the end of the Throw Out, the lead should adjust, if necessary, to face the follow squarely.

LEAD: On count 2, the lead pulls down with his left hand, guiding the follow out.

NOTE: The Throw Out may be used as a prep step for many variations, or the couple may return to Social Swing position.

RETURNING TO SOCIAL SWING OUT POSITION

STEPS	4/4 COUNTS	STEP CUE
Lead's Part		
Step L back, next to R	+	together
Step R in place	1	place
Pivot on R 45° clockwise, side step L on L foot	2	side
Step R in place	3	place
Follow's Part		
Step R back, next to L	+	together
Step L forward	1	forward
Step R forward	2	forward
Pivot on R 180° clockwise, step L back	3	turn

LEAD: The lead pulls down with his left hand to guide the follow next to him. The lead replaces his right hand on the follow's back by count 3.

LEAD'S UNDERARM PASS

(Swing Out position)

The lead veers to the left while he goes under the follow's arm, as the follow passes behind.

STEPS	4/4 COUNTS	STEP CUE
Lead's Part		
Step L back, next to R	+	together
Step R forward	1	forward
Step diagonal forward L on L	2	under
Pivot on L 180° counterclockwise, step R back	3	back
Follow's Part		
Step R back, next to L	+	together
Step L forward	1	forward
Step R forward	2	forward
Pivot on R 180° counterwise, step L back	3	turn

STYLE: The free arms are extended out to the side as the lead goes under the arm.

LEAD: The lead lifts his left arm and gently guides the folllow behind him as he goes under her arm.

NOTE: This move is usually done two times in a row.

Charleston

The Roaring Twenties saw the advent of Dixieland jazz and the *Charleston*. Definitely a fad dance, the Charleston comes and goes, only to reappear again. The dance, with its fancy footwork and carefree abandon, is a challenge to young and old. Black dock workers of Charleston, South Carolina, are credited with performing the dance steps eventually referred to as the Charleston. In 1923, the Ziegfeld Follies popularized the step in a show called "Running Wild." Teachers toned the kicking steps down and interspersed them with the Two-Step and Foxtrot, and the United States had a new popular dance. The *Varsity Drag* was one of many dances that incorporated the basic Charleston step. The dance permitted individuals to express their ability with many Charleston variations, independent of their partner.

CHARLESTON RHYTHM

The Charleston rhythm is written in 4/4 time. The bouncy quality of the music occurs in the shift of accent, becoming a highly syncopated rhythm.

```
     /    /  /  /  /
4/4  Q | Q Q Q Q Q Q Q Q
     —   — — — — — — — —
     —   — — — — — — — —
     &  | 1 & 2 & 3 & 4 &
```

The rhythm is an even beat pattern of quicks counted *"and 1, and 2, and 3, and 4."* The knee bends on the *and* before the step. It is the *and* that gives the Charleston its characteristic bounce. Rhythmically, the beats are:

The accent shifts from the first beat to the eighth note tied to the third beat, which gives punch to the rhythm. The rhythm is jerky, staccato, and syncopated.

CHARLESTON STYLE

The twisting of the feet and the bending of the knees before each step, then the straightening of the leg, are basic. The arms move in opposition to the feet: For example, step left, point right and swing both arms across to the left, step right, point left, and swing arms across right. The Charleston may be danced as a solo; in a line with a group; or with a partner, side by side, on the same foot, or facing each other, hands joined or closed position.

■ *Charleston with Partner*

Partners may be (a) side by side, on the same foot, (b) facing each other, hands joined, or (c) closed position. The lead is visual. The lead starts with his left, follow right. Any step changes start with lead's left. Lead and follow stop together.

TEACHING SUGGESTIONS

1. Practice rhythm first. Feet slightly apart and parallel, bend knees (*and*), straighten legs (count 1). Repeat the action of "*and* 1, *and* 2, *and* 3, *and* 4." Then add the music.
2. Practice pivot on balls of feet. Heels out (*and*), heels in (count 1). Repeat.
3. *Charleston Twist.* Combine **1** and **2**. Bend knees and heels out (*and*), straighten legs and heels in (count 1). Repeat.
4. Add arm movement, swinging arms in opposition to feet. Swinging arms helps to maintain balance.
5. If balance and timing are difficult, try sitting on the edge of a chair to establish the rhythm; then stand behind the chair, holding onto the back for support.
6. Teach all figures in place. Then move forward and backward. Practice without music, slowly. If record player has a variable speed, introduce music as soon as possible. Gradually increase tempo until the correct tempo is reached.

FUNDAMENTAL CHARLESTON STEPS

RECORD: "The Golden Age of the Charleston," EMI Records LTD., GX 2507; or any good recording of the 1920s.

FORMATION: Free formation, all facing music.

POINT STEP
(Feet together, weight on R)

STEPS	4/4 COUNTS	DIRECTION CUE
Bend R knee	*and*	*and*
Step forward L	1	step forward
Bend L knee	*and*	*and*
Point R toe forward, straighten knees	2	point forward
Bend L knee	*and*	*and*
Step back R	3	step back
Bend R knee	*and*	*and*
Point L toe back, straighten knees	4	point forward

ARMS: Swing arms in opposition to legs. Right toe forward, left arm swings forward, right arm swings back; left toe forward, right arm swings forward, left arm swings back.

SINGLE KICK STEP
(Feet together, weight on R)

STEPS	4/4 COUNTS	DIRECTION CUE
Bend R knee	*and*	*and*
Step forward L	1	step forward
Bend L knee	*and*	*and*
Kick R leg forward, straighten knees	2	kick forward
Bend L knee	*and*	*and*
Step back R	3	step back
Bend R knee	*and*	*and*
Kick L leg back	4	kick back
Straighten knees	*and*	*and*

ARMS: Swing arms in opposition to the kick. Kick right leg forward, left arm swings forward, right arm swings back; kick left leg forward, right arm swings forward, left arm swings back.

■ *Variations*

1. *Double Kick.* Step forward left; kick right forward, then backward; step right in place. Repeat kicking left forward, then backward; step left.
2. *Single Diagonal Kick.* Step sideward left, kick diagonally forward across left leg, step sideward right, kick diagonally forward across right leg.

CHARLESTON TWIST

(Weight on the balls of both feet, heels touching, toes pointing out)

1. The twist comes from pivoting on balls of feet, heels turned out, then pivoting on balls of feet, heels turned in. Heels are slightly off the floor to allow the pivot action.

STEPS	4/4 COUNTS	DIRECTION CUE
Bend knees, pivot in on balls of feet	*and*	heels out
Pivot out, straighten knees	1	heels in
Repeat over and over.		

2. Twist and snap (heels touching, toes pointing out, weight on right).

STEPS	4/4 COUNTS	DIRECTION CUE
Bend R knee, pivot in on ball of foot, lifting L leg up, knee turned in	*and*	heel out
Pivot out on ball of R foot; straighten knees; place L foot by heel of R, toe pointed out; L takes weight	1	heel in
Bend L knee; pivot in on ball of foot, lifting L leg up, knee turned in	*and*	heel out
Pivot out on ball of L foot, straighten knees, place R foot by heel of L, toe pointed out; R takes weight	2	heel in

JUMP

STEPS	4/4 COUNTS	DIRECTION CUE
Bend both knees together	*and*	bend
Jump forward diagonally L, both arms swing L, shoulder height	1	jump
Bend both knees	*and*	bend
Jump back, both arms swing down	2	jump
Repeat jump and arms forward and back	*and 1 and 2*	
Bend both knees together	*and*	
Jump forward diagonally R, both arms swing R, shoulder height	1	jump
Bend both knees together	*and*	
Jump back, both arms swing down	2	jump
Repeat jump and arms forward and back	*and 1 and 2*	jump jump
Alternately jump L R L R, arms swing L R L R	*and 1 and 2*	jump

SWIVEL

Weight on heel, pivot toes right (count *and*); weight on toes, pivot heels right (count 1). Continue to move right, heel, toe, heel, toe. Arms swing left and down, repeating with heel, toe. Travel on counts and 1 and 2. Reverse movement to travel left.

SUZY Q

Pivoting on left heel and right toe simultaneously (count *and*), then pivoting on left toe and right heel simultaneously (count 1). Continue alternating, traveling right. Hands in front of chest, elbows out as heels are apart; drop elbows as toes are apart; alternate elbows out and dropped with foot movement. Reverse footwork to travel left.

TWELFTH STREET RAG

Composed Charleston Dance in Line Dance.

Tango

The *TANGO* BEGAN as a raw, sensuous dance born on the Rio de la Plata in Buenos Aires amid the slums in a multiracial setting. In its earliest form, the name *tangoo*, an onomatopoetic rendition of the sounds of drums, strongly suggest its African origin. As with all dance forms, the Tango has passed through many evolutions. During its formative stages, it was a combination of *Candombe*, a syncopated African dance, the *Habanera*, an eighteenth century European dance, and the *Milango*, an indigenous Argentine dance.

The Tango and its music was introduced to Paris and the Riviera by wealthy South Americans after World War I. It became the rage of Paris, and it is from this setting and refinement that it spread throughout Europe and came to North America.

The 1990s have become the new age of the Tango. *Tangueros* are found in major cities around the world. Devotees attend workshops, organize weekly dances, and practice to improve their skills while exchanging feelings and excitement about dancing the Argentine Tango. While maintaining its smooth, sophisticated, and suave style, the Tango's new charm lies in its improvised nature that relies on communication between partners rather than executing prelearned step routines.

TANGO RHYTHM

The modern Tango is written in both 2/4 and 4/4 time. Here it will be presented 2/4 time.

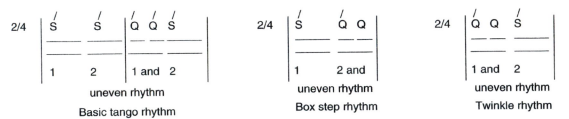

The Tango rhythm is a deliberate accented beat that is easily distinguished. Few dancers have trouble following the Tango rhythm. There is a calculated contrast between the slow promenade beats of the first measure and the staccato of the Tango break in the second measure.

TANGO STYLE

The Tango is characterized by a deliberate glide, not sliding the foot on the floor, but a long reach from the hip with a catlike smoothness and placement of the ball of the foot on the floor. The knees remain straight. The break, which is quick quick slow, is a sudden contrast ending in the subtle draw of the feet together. It is this combination of slow gliding beats and the sharp break that makes the Tango distinctive. Restraint is achieved by the use of continuous flow of movements and a controlled, stylized break presenting disciplined and sophisticated style, instead of a comic caricature. The dancer should strive to effect the idea of floating. Care should be taken to avoid the look of stiffness. Since the long reaching glide is used, the feet should pass each other close together. The draw in the Tango close is executed slowly, taking the full length of the slow beat to bring the feet together and then sweep quickly into the beginning of the basic rhythm again. The follow should synchronize the action of her drawing step with that of the lead. The body and head are carried high and the follow's left hand, instead of being on the lead's shoulder as in other dances, reaches around the lead at his right shoulder–blade level. The fingers of the hand are straight, and the arm is in a straight line from the elbow to the tip of the fingers.

Once in a while, deliberately move the shoulders forward in opposition to the feet. For example, stepping left, the right shoulder moves forward. The fan steps, most glamorous of all Tango patterns, turn, whip, or swirl in an exciting, subtle way. The fan style is described in detail with the variations used.

FUNDAMENTAL TANGO STEPS

Directions are for the lead, facing the line of direction; the follow's part is reversed, except as noted.

BASIC TANGO STEP
(Closed position)

A combination of the promenade or walking step and the break.

STEPS	2/4 COUNTS	RHYTHM CUE
Step L forward	1	slow
Step R forward	2	slow
Step L forward	1	quick
Step R sideward abruptly	*and*	quick
Draw L to R, weight remains on R	2	slow

STEP CUE: Slow slow Tango close.
       S   S   QQ   S

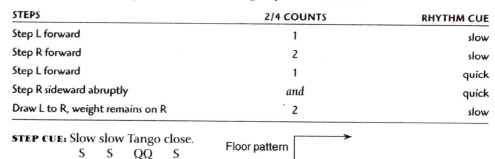

Floor pattern

start

STYLE: The slow beats are long, smooth, gliding steps. The feet pass each other closely. The break quick quick slow is in place or slightly forward.

LEAD: Lead must draw to the right with right hand and elbow to guide the follow in the break step.

NOTE: This step repeats each time from the lead's left foot, because there is no change of weight on the draw. This pattern will tend to carry the couple outward toward the wall. It immediately becomes necessary to know how to vary the step in order to counteract this action. Open position, right parallel position, or quarter–turn all may be used for this purpose.

■ Tango Step Variations

Promenade	Half–Turn Counterclockwise	The Corté
Right Parallel Basic Tango	Half–Turn Clockwise	Preparation Step
Quarter–Turn	Double Cross	
Cross Step & Quarter–Turn	The Box Step	

PROMENADE
(Closed position)

STEPS	2/4 COUNTS	RHYTHM CUE
Step L into open position, turning abruptly	1	slow
Step R forward, in open position	2	slow
Step L forward, a short step, pivoting on L foot abruptly to face partner in closed position	1	quick
Step R sideward, in closed position	*and*	quick
Draw L to R, no change of weight	2	slow

STEP CUE: Open step close side draw.

STYLE: The abrupt turning to open position on the first slow step and the turn back to closed position are sharp and only a firmness in the body can accomplish this.

LEAD: Refer to leads 7 and 8, p. 14. The lead is sudden and on the first slow beat.

RIGHT PARALLEL BASIC TANGO
(Closed position)

STEPS	2/4 COUNTS	RHYTHM CUE
Step L diagonally into R parallel position turning abruptly	1	slow
Step R forward	2	slow
Step L, a short step forward, turning abruptly to closed dance position	1	quick
Step R sideward	*and*	quick
Draw L to R, no change of weight	2	slow

STEP CUE: Parallel step close side draw.

STYLE: Right parallel travels diagonally forward; follow's foot reaches parallel to lead's left foot. The second slow is an exaggerated reaching step forward.

LEAD: To lead into right parallel position (left reverse open position) the lead should not use pressure of his right hand, but rather should raise his right arm rotating the follow counterclockwise one–eighth of a turn while he rotates counterclockwise one–eighth of a turn. This places the lead and follow off to the side of each other facing opposite directions. The follow is to the right of the lead, but slightly in front of him. The lead should avoid turning too far so as to be side by side as this results in poor style and awkward and uncomfortable motion. The lead's left hand may assist the lead by pulling toward his left shoulder.

QUARTER-TURN

(Closed position)

STEPS	2/4 COUNTS	RHYTHM CUE
Step L forward	1	slow
Step R forward	2	slow
Step L, turning one-quarter counterclockwise	1	quick
Step R sideward	*and*	quick
Draw L to R, no change of weight	2	slow

CROSS STEP AND QUARTER-TURN

(Closed position)

STEPS	2/4 COUNTS	RHYTHM CUE
Step L sideward	1	slow
Step R across in front of L, take weight R	2	slow
Step L sideward, turn toe out, turn one-quarter counterclockwise	1	quick
Step R sideward	*and*	quick
Draw L to R, no change of weight	2	slow

STEP CUE: Side cross turn side close.

STYLE: All of this pattern is taken in closed position. The turn actually begins by a pivot on the crossing foot at the end of the second slow beat.

LEAD: Refer to lead 12, p. 14.

HALF-TURN COUNTERCLOCKWISE

(Closed position)

STEPS	2/4 COUNTS	RHYTHM CUE
Step L into open position, turning abruptly	1	slow
Step R forward, a short step, pivoting one-quarter counterclockwise on the R foot; bring up R arm and turn the follow around the lead a three-quarter turn to closed position	2	slow
Step L bringing L foot next to R foot	1	quick
Step R sideward	*and*	quick
Draw L to R, no weight change	2	slow

STEP CUE: Step pivot break side draw.

STYLE: The follow pivots counterclockwise on her left foot (second slow beat) around the lead a three-quarter turn into closed position. The follow's step on this beat is a longer step than the lead's, giving her freedom to pivot. She must bring her first quick step with right foot alongside of left foot.

LEAD: Lead must bring up his right arm and elbow firmly, almost lifting her so that she can pivot easily on her left foot on the second slow beat.

HALF-TURN CLOCKWISE

(Closed position)

STEPS	2/4 COUNTS	RHYTHM CUE
Step L into open position, turning abruptly	1	slow
Step R forward, a long step, pivoting one–half clockwise on the R foot around the follow into closed position	2	slow
Step L sideward, a short step apart from where R foot is at the end of the pivot	1	quick
Step R sideward	*and*	quick
Draw L to R, no weight change	2	slow

STEP CUE: Step pivot break side draw.

STYLE: The lead smoothly pivots on his right foot clockwise about halfway around the follow. The follow turns clockwise in place on her left foot. This step is very easy for the follow.

LEAD: Refer to lead indications 7 and 8, p. 14, for open and closed position. The main lead is increased resistance in hand, arm, and body as the lead pivots halfway around the follow.

DOUBLE CROSS

(In twinkle rhythm, closed position)

STEPS	2/4 COUNTS	RHYTHM CUE
Step L sideways	1	slow
Step R across in front of L	2	slow
Point L sideways, take weight slightly	1	quick
Pivot hips to R with a slight push off with L, take weight R	*and*	quick
Swing L across in front of R, take weight L	2	slow
Point R to side	1	quick
Pivot hips to L with slight push off with R, take weight L	*and*	quick
Swing R across in front of L, take weight R	2	slow

STEP CUE: Side cross pivot and cross pivot and cross.
                   S   S   Q   Q   S   Q   Q   S

STYLE: Stay in closed position throughout. Follow crosses in front, also.

LEAD: Firm body and arm control are needed to hold closed position.

NOTE: Finish with break side draw quick quick slow. This could also be done with the follow crossing behind.

THE BOX STEP

The rhythm of the Tango box step is like that described in the Foxtrot—slow quick quick—forward side close, back side close. The Tango gliding action will be used on the first slow beat. The box step variations for Foxtrot may also be used here, including the box turn and the grapevine step. Refer to pp. 32, 33, and 35.

THE CORTÉ

The corté is a dip, most often taken backward on the lead's left or right foot. It is a type of break step used to finish off almost any Tango variation and is used as an ending to the dance. The skilled dancer will learn to use the corté in relationship to the music of the tango so that the feeling of the corté will correspond to the climax or the phrase of the musical accompaniment.

The left corté will be described here. A right corté may be taken by starting on the right foot and reversing the pattern. A preliminary step is nearly always used as a preparation for going into the corté. It is described here as a part of the rhythm of the corté.

PREPARATION STEP

STEPS	2/4 COUNTS	RHYTHM CUE
Step forward L, a short step	1	quick
Shift weight back onto R	*and*	quick

Corté

STEPS	2/4 COUNTS	RHYTHM CUE
Step L backward, take weight, and bend L knee slightly	2	slow
Recover forward, take weight R	1	slow
Step L in place beside R	2	quick
Step R in place beside L	*and*	quick

STEP CUE: Rock and dip recover quick quick.
　　　　　　 Q　 Q　 S　　 S　　 Q　　 Q

STYLE: As the *lead* steps backward into the corté, the weight is all taken on the standing foot with a bent knee. The lead should turn his bent knee slightly outward so that the follow's knee will not bump his as they go into the dip. His left shoulder and arm move forward (the left leg and left shoulder are in opposition). His back should remain straight. He should avoid leaning either backward or forward. His right foot should be extended (arched) so that the toe is only touching the floor.

The *follow* should step forward on the right, arch her back, and place all of her weight over the forward right foot. The right knee is bent. The left leg is extended behind and should be a straight line from hip to toe. A bent line makes the whole figure sag. The left arch of the foot should be extended so that the toe is pointed and remains in contact with the floor. If the follow steps forward too far or does not bend the forward knee, she will be forced to bend at the waist, which destroys the form of the figure. She may look back over her left shoulder. The execution of the dip should be as smooth as any slow backward step.

The lead should avoid leaping or falling back into the dip.

LEAD: The left shoulder leads forward as the lead goes into the preparation step on the first beat. There is an increase of tension of the lead's right arm and hand also on the first beat, plus general resistance throughout the upper body. The lead will draw the follow with his right arm when stepping into the dip and release on the recovery step. The lead is essential for the corté as the pattern cannot be executed correctly unless both lead and follow are completely on balance and ready for it.

NOTE: The recovery step is followed by two quick steps left right, which finish on count 2 and complete the measure of music. These may be omitted when they follow a variation that takes up those extra counts. Learn the footwork first, then work on the style.

■ *Fan Step*

The *fan* is a term used to describe a manner of executing a leg motion, in which the free leg swings in a whiplike movement around a small pivoting base. This should not be a large sweeping movement in a wide arc but rather a small subtle action initiated in the hip and executed with the legs close together. The balance is carefully poised over the pivoting foot at all times. When the lead and follow take the fan motion, the action is taken parallel to partner; that is, the right leg, which is free, swings forward. When it reaches its full extension, just barely off the floor, the right hip turns the leg over, knee down, while pivoting on the standing foot to face the opposite direction. The right leg then swings through forward and the weight is taken on the right foot. This action usually is done in slow rhythm. Accompanying the hip action there is also a lift and turn on the ball of the standing foot. This lift permits the free leg to swing through gracefully extended and close in a beautiful floating style.

OPEN FAN

(Open position)

STEPS	2/4 COUNTS	RHYTHM CUE
Step L forward	1	slow
Step R forward	2	slow
Step L in place, releasing R arm around follow, and turn halfway around to the right to a side-by-side position with follow on lead's L	1	quick
Step R sideward, a short step	*and*	quick
Draw L to R, no weight change (the lead's L hand is holding the follow's R)	2	slow
Step forward L	1	quick
Swing the R leg forward, pivoting on L foot while fanning the R, coming halfway around to open position	*and*	quick
Step forward R in open position	2	slow
Step L forward, pivoting toward the follow into closed position	1	quick
Step R sideward	*and*	quick
Draw L to R, no weight change	2	slow

STEP CUE: Slow slow open side draw/fan through break side draw.

STYLE: When the lead releases his arm around her, the follow turns halfway around to the left. On the fan, the follow steps right, swings left leg forward, hip turns over, knee faces down. Foot is kept close to the floor and sweeps through pivoting clockwise to open position, and weight is transferred forward onto left foot. She then goes into break step with partner.

LEAD: The lead drops his right arm and pulls away from the follow to side–by–side position. Then, with his left hand, he pulls in as he fans through to open position and from there lifts his right arm into closed position for Tango close.

NOTE: This is an easy beginner step in fan style and gives them the thrill of the Tango.

GRAPEVINE FAN

(Starting in open position)

STEPS	2/4 COUNTS	RHYTHM CUE
Step L forward	1	slow
Rock forward and back R, L	2 and	quick quick
Step R backward rising on R toe and lifting L leg just off the floor	1	slow
Step L backward, turning toward partner	2	quick
Step R sideward, turning to face reverse open position	and	quick
Step L forward in reverse open position	1	quick
Fan R leg forward and through to open position	and	quick
Step R forward, in open position	2	slow
Step L forward, a short step, turning to closed position	1	quick
Step R sideward	and	quick
Draw L to R, no weight change	2	slow

STEP CUE: Step rock and back grapevine step fan through break side close.
     S   Q   Q   S   Q   Q   Q   Q   S   Q   Q   S

STYLE: The couple should not get too far apart or lean forward to maneuver this grapevine pattern. They should stand upright and keep carefully balanced over standing foot. The fanning leg swings in line with the travelling and facing action, not in a side arc. The legs are kept close together.

LEAD: This is a pattern lead and follow must know together but the lead cues the follow by use of both hands and use of his body in turning from one position to another.

NOTE: This is a beautiful pattern when used following the forward and open rock.

PARALLEL FAN

(Fan style in parallel position; starting in closed position)

STEPS	2/4 COUNTS	RHYTHM CUE
Lead's Part: Starts and ends in closed position. Starting L, take one basic Tango step, slow slow quick quick slow		
Step L forward	1	slow
Step R sideward turning to open position	2	quick
Step L to R, taking weight L	and	quick
Step R forward, turning follow to R parallel position	1	slow
Rock backward onto L, turning follow to open position	2	slow
Rock forward onto R, turning follow to R parallel position	1	slow
Rock back onto L, turning follow to open position	2	slow
Step R forward in open position	1	slow
Take Tango—close step, turning to closed position	2 and 1	quick quick slow

Follow's Part: *Starting right, take one basic tango step, slow slow quick quick slow.*

Step R backward	1	slow
Step L sideward, turning to open position	2	quick
Step R to L, taking weight on R	*and*	quick
Step L forward (fan), pivoting to R parallel position	1	slow
Step R forward (fan), pivoting to open position	2	slow
Step L forward (fan), pivoting to R parallel position	1	slow
Step R forward (fan), pivoting to open position	2	slow
Step L forward (fan), pivoting to R parallel position	1	slow
Step R forward (fan), pivoting to open position	2	slow
Step L forward, turning to closed position	1	slow
Take Tango close	2 and 1	quick quick slow

STEP CUE: With slow and quick rhythm except for the fan: rock rock rock rock/forward break side draw.

STYLE: The steps are small in the fan part of the step so that the follow may turn without reaching for the step. The lead in the fan part of the step rocks forward, back, forward, back in place, as he turns the follow. She takes her fan, pivoting alternately on the left, right, left, right, swinging the free leg forward a short distance until the toe just clears the floor and then turning the hip with her pivot to the new direction and reaching through for the next step. The follow should rise slightly on her toe as she pivots. This smooths out the turn and makes one of the most beautiful movements in Tango.

LEAD: The lead's first lead will be to lower right arm into open position. He then guides her forward with his right hand, moving her alternately from right parallel position to open position until the end when he raises his right arm and turns her to closed position.

NOTE: A corté may be added to this figure instead of the Tango close by stepping through to open position on the right (count 1), turning the follow quickly to closed position, rocking forward and back (counts 2 *and*); corté (count 1), recover onto the left foot (count 2) and finish with Tango close (counts 1 and 2).

TANGO COMBOS

The Tango routines are combinations for practice, listed from simple to complex. (Closed position, unless otherwise indicated.)

1. *Basic*
   2 basic steps
   1 promenade
2. *Basic, Cross Step*
   2 basic steps
   4 cross steps and quarter–turn
3. *Box, Basic, Cross Step*
   2 box steps
   1 basic step
   1 cross step and quarter–turn

4. *Basic, Cross, Corté*
   2 basics
   1 cross step, quarter–turn
   1 corté
5. *Advanced Combo*
   2 box steps
   1 basic
   1 cross step
   open fan

6. *Advanced Combo*
   2 basics
   open fan
   half–turn clockwise
   corté
   1 basic

Waltz

Although a majority of the middle European countries lay some claim to the origin of the *Waltz*, the world looked to Germany and Austria, where the great Waltz was made traditional by the beautiful music of Johann Strauss and his sons. It has a pulsating, swinging rhythm, which has been enjoyed by dancers everywhere, even by those who dance it only in its simplest pattern, the Waltz Turn. Its immediate popularity and its temporary obscurity are not unlike other fine inheritances of the past, which come and go with the ebb and flow of popular accord. Early use of the Waltz in America was at the elegant social balls and cotillions. Its outstanding contribution to present–day dancing is the Waltz position. Even in its early stages, it was quite some time before this position was socially acceptable. Now the closed position is universally the basic position for Ballroom Dancing.

The Waltz music is played in three different tempos—slow, medium, and fast. The slow or medium Waltz is preferred by most people. However, the fast Waltz is a favorite of those who know the Viennese style. The slower American style is danced for the most part on a box pattern, but the use of other variations has added a new interest.

WALTZ RHYTHM

The Waltz is played in 3/4 time. It is three beats per measure of music, with an accent on the first beat. The three beats of Waltz time are very even, each beat receiving the same amount of time. The three movements of the Waltz step pattern blend perfectly with the musical tempo or beat of each measure. The tempo may be slow, medium, or fast.

3/4 | slow slow slow
1   2   3
even rhythm
Slow box rhythm

Canter rhythm in Waltz time is a means of holding the first and second beats together so the resultant pattern is an uneven rhythm, or slow quick slow quick. It is counted 1, 3, 1, 3.

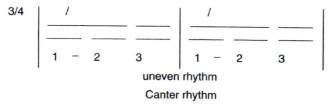

3/4 | 1 — 2   3 | 1 — 2   3 |
uneven rhythm
Canter rhythm

The Viennese Waltz is an even three–beat rhythm, played very fast. It is a turning pattern. There is only one step on the first beat of the measure and a pivot of the body on that foot for the two remaining counts of the measure.

```
        /
3/4 | step    pivot    _____
    |
    | _____  _____   _____
    |
    |  1        2        3
           even rhythm
      Viennese rhythm
```

WALTZ STYLE

The Waltz is a smooth dance with a gliding quality that weaves an even pattern of swinging and turning movement. The first accented beat of the music is also accented in the motion. The first step of the Waltz pattern is the reaching step forward, back-ward, sideward, or turning. Because it is the first beat that gives the dance its new impetus, its new direction, or a change of step, there evolves a pulsating feeling, which can be seen rather markedly and is the chief characteristic of the beauty of the Waltz. This should not be interpreted as a rocking or bobbing motion of the body. On count 1, the lead steps *flat* on the sole of the foot; on counts 2–3, his body rises stepping on the ball of the foot. The rising action is sometimes described as a *lift*. The "fall and rise" action of the body is seen in every step. The footwork is most effective when the foot taking the second beat glides past the standing foot as it moves into the sideward step. The feet should never be heard to scrape the floor, but should seem to float in a silent pattern. In closed position, it is important for the follow to be directly in front of the lead, their shoulders parallel.

FUNDAMENTAL WALTZ STEPS

Directions are for the lead, facing line of direction; follow's part is reversed, except as noted.

BOX STEP
(Closed position)

STEPS	3/4 COUNTS	STYLE CUE
Step L forward	1	flat
Step R sideward, passing close to the L foot	2	lift
Close L to R, take weight L	3	lift
Step R backward	1	flat
Step L sideward, passing close to the R foot	2	lift
Close R to L, take weight R	3	lift

STEP CUE: Forward side close/back side close.

STYLE: The forward step is *on the heel*. Follow through on the second beat, moving the free foot closely past the standing foot, but do not lose a beat by stopping. Body rises on counts 2, 3 as stepping on ball of foot. The floor pattern is a long narrow rectangle rather than a square box.

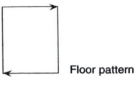
Floor pattern

LEAD: To lead a box step the lead should use a forward body action followed by right-hand pressure and right elbow pull to the right to take the follow into the forward sequence of the box. Forward pressure of the right hand followed by pressure to the left side takes the follow into the back sequence of the box.

NOTE: The lead must understand the concept of the forward side close as being the forward sequence of the box and the backward side close as being the back sequence of the box. This terminology will be used in future patterns.

BOX TURN

(Left) (Closed position)

STEPS	3/4 COUNTS	STYLE CUE
Step L forward, toe out, turning one-quarter L	1	flat
Step R sideward, gliding past the L foot	2	lift
Close L to R, taking weight L	3	lift
Step R backward, toe in, turning one-quarter L	1	flat
Step L sideward, gliding past the R foot	2	lift
Close R to L, taking weight R	3	lift
Step L forward, toe out, turning one-quarter L	1	flat
Step R sideward, gliding past the L foot	2	lift
Close L to R, taking weight on L	3	lift
Step R backward, toe in, turning one-quarter L	1	flat
Step L sideward, gliding past the R foot	2	lift
Close R to L, taking weight R	3	lift

STEP CUE: Turn side close, turn side close.

FOLLOW: The follow is taking the reverse pattern, except that, when the follow steps forward with the left foot, instead of toeing out as described for the lead, she steps forward between the lead's feet, her left foot next to the instep of the lead's left foot. This style greatly facilitates the turn.

LEAD: A common error is that the lead tries to step around his partner. The follow must be directly in front of her partner.

STYLE: Accent the first step by reaching with a longer step. However, the lead must be careful not to overreach his partner. There is no unnecessary knee bending or bobbing up and down.

LEAD: To lead a box turn with slight pressure of the right hand, the lead should use the right arm and shoulder to guide or bank the follow into the turn. The shoulders press forward during the forward step and draw backward during the backward step.

NOTE: For the right turn, start with the right foot. Follow the same pattern with opposite footwork.

TRAVELING BOX

(Closed position)

Use this step to travel around the dance floor in the line of direction.

STEPS	3/4 COUNTS	STYLE CUE
Step L forward	1	forward
Step R side	2	rise
Close L to R, taking weight L	3	lower
Step R forward	1	forward
Step L side	2	rise
Close R to L, taking weight R	3	lower

STYLE: The first three counts are exactly like the Basic Box step. On count 2 of the second part, the lead must step forward, in between the follow's feet, not outside.

LEAD: The lead has a forward body action on count 1 of the second part, guiding the follow in line of direction. If the lead hesitates, the follow will start to move in the back sequence of the box step.

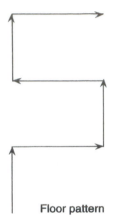

Floor pattern

■ Teaching Strategy for Changing Leads—Turn Right, Turn Left

It is important to learn to turn counterclockwise and clockwise. The foot must be free to *lead* in the direction of the turn: left lead for left turn; right lead for right turn. There are several ways to change the lead. With the left, step balance or a hesitation step, then start the box with the right foot (right side close, left side close). Another is to take two Waltz steps forward, take the third Waltz step backward; right foot is now free to turn right. To return to the left lead, either step (Right) balance or take two Waltz steps forward and the third one backward; then the left foot leads again. Once the student can turn left and right, the teacher should present a definite routine that drills this change. When students learn this concept for the Waltz, they will be able to transfer the principle to other rhythms.

■ Waltz Step Variations

Hesitation Step	Weaving Step	Streamline Step
Cross Step	Twinkle Step	Viennese Waltz

HESITATION STEP
(Closed position)

STEPS	3/4 COUNTS	STYLE CUE
Step L forward	1	flat
Bring R foot up to the instep of L and hold, no weight change	2, 3	lift
Step R backward	1	flat
Bring L foot up to the instep of R foot, no weight change	2, 3	lift

STEP CUE: Step close hold.

STYLE: Smooth.

LEAD: To lead a hesitation step the lead dips his shoulder in the direction of the turn, and his upper torso turns before his leg and foot turn.

NOTE: As in the Foxtrot, a beautiful combination is to dance two hesitation steps, then the first half of the box turn, two hesitation steps and then the second half of the turn. The hesitation step repeated may also be done turning either counterclockwise or clockwise and may be useful in maneuvering for the next step.

CROSS STEP

(Closed position)

STEPS	3/4 COUNTS	STYLE CUE
Step L forward	1	flat
Step R sideward, turning to open position	2	lift
Close L to R, taking weight L	3	lift
Step R forward, in open position	1	flat
Step L forward, turning on L foot to face partner in closed position	2	lift
Close R to L, taking weight R	3	lift

STEP CUE: Forward side close, cross side close.

STYLE: The position is opened to semiopen position, just enough to step forward on the inside foot, which feels like a crossing step. It should be accented by a long, smooth, reaching step on the heel, not a dipping or bobbing action.

LEAD: To lead into an open position or conversation position, the lead should use pressure with the heel of the right hand to turn the follow into open position. The right elbow lowers to the side. The lead must simultaneously turn his own body, not just the follow so that they end facing the same direction. The left arm relaxes slightly, and the left hand sometimes gives the lead for steps in the open position.

LEAD: To lead from open to closed position, the lead should use pressure of the right hand and raise the right arm up to standard position to move the follow into closed position. The follow should not have to be pushed but should swing easily into closed position as she feels the arm lifting. She should move completely around to face the lead squarely.

NOTE: When the lead is facing out in closed position, he can go into this step and the cross pattern will travel in line of direction.

WEAVING STEP

(Same as cross step but crossing from side to side) (Closed position)

STEPS	3/4 COUNTS	STYLE CUE
Step L forward	1	flat
Step R sideward, turning to open position	2	lift
Close L to R, taking weight L	3	lift
Step R forward in open position	1	flat
Step L forward, turning to side-by-side position facing the reverse line of direction	2	lift
Close R to L, taking weight R	3	lift
Step L forward, in side-by-side position	1	flat
Step R forward, turning to open position	2	lift
Close L to R, taking weight L	3	lift
Step R forward in open position	1	flat
Step L forward, turning to closed position	2	lift
Close R to L, taking weight R	3	lift

STEP CUE: Forward side open, cross side reverse, cross side reverse, cross side close.

STYLE: Reach into crossing step on the heel. It is a long reaching step on the accented beat.

LEAD: Turn follow to semiopen position for first cross step and then drop right arm and lead through with the left hand to side–by–side position, facing the reverse line of direction. Next time, as they reverse direction, the lead puts his arm around her in open position and follows standard procedure for returning to closed position.

NOTE: The weave pattern may be repeated back and forth, crossing as many times as desired, but should go back to closed position as described above.

TWINKLE STEP

(Closed position)

It is led from the back sequence of the box step.

STEPS	3/4 COUNTS	STYLE CUE
Step L forward	1	flat
Step R sideward turning into R parallel position	2	lift
Close L to R, taking eight L	3	lift
Step R, diagonally forward in R parallel position	1	flat
Step L sideward, turning from R parallel to L parallel position	2	lift
Close R to L, taking weight R	3	lift
Step L diagonally forward in L parallel position	1	flat
Step R sideward, turning from L parallel position to R parallel position	2	lift
Close L to R, taking weight on L	3	lift
Step R diagonally forward in R parallel position	1	flat
Step L sideward turning to closed position	2	lift
Close R to L, taking weight on R	3	lift

Floor pattern

start

STEP CUE: Step turn close. The second beat has a short step and a smooth roll from one position to another. The follow reaches parallel to the lead's step, except that she is stepping diagonally backward, which takes a lot of practice for the follow to do it well.

LEAD: To lead into right parallel position the lead should not use pressure of his right hand, but rather should raise his right arm rotating the follow counterclockwise one–eighth of a turn while he rotates counterclockwise one–eighth of a turn. This places the lead and follow off to the side of each other facing opposite directions. The follow is to the right of the lead but slightly in front of him. The lead should avoid turning too far so as to be side by side as this results in poor style and awkward and uncomfortable motion. The lead's left hand may assist the lead by pulling toward his left shoulder.

LEAD: To lead from right parallel position to left parallel position the lead should pull with his right hand lowering the right arm and push slightly with his left hand causing a rotation clockwise about a quarter of a turn until the follow is to the left of him but slightly in front of him. They are not side by side.

NOTE: Progress is in a zigzag pattern down the floor in the line of direction and may repeat over and over as desired.

■ *Suggestions for Variations*

Any student or teacher who has followed these directions this far should be prepared to make use of the advance twinkle, corté, and pivot turn described under the Foxtrot by transposing a slow, quick, quick in 4/4 time into slow, slow, slow in 3/4 time. Refer to corté p. 31, Twinkle p. 34, Pivot Turn p. 36.

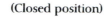

STREAMLINE STEP

(Closed position)

An advanced step seen in the International Style and competition. Dancers travel in the line of direction and need a lot of space to move. Step on every beat, each step forward. The feet are never together, always moving forward! Step flat on the first beat; body rises on counts 2–3. The floor pattern, although forward, zigs and zags. In addition to moving forward, the dancers may rock or grapevine.

ROCK: Forward, backward, forward; backward, forward, backward.

GRAPEVINE: Semiopen position, travel in line of direction.

VIENNESE WALTZ

The rhythm is three even, quick beats now instead of slow. The Viennese Waltz music is fast and it is hard to keep one's balance on the pivot step when it is slowed down, so that students get discouraged learning the step. An experiment of a half-Viennese has proved successful in getting students to learn the pivot step by doing it first on the right foot and then taking a regular Waltz step on the left sequence.

3/4	step	side	cross	step	pivot	
	1	2	3	1	2	3
	quick	quick	quick	right	pivot	

Half-Viennese step

Half–Viennese Step: Both lead and follow need to practice this pattern alone, traveling down line of direction.

STEPS	3/4 COUNTS	RHYTHM CUE
Step L forward, turning one-quarter counterclockwise	1	quick
Step R sideward, turning one-quarter counterclockwise	2	quick
Slide the L foot, heel first, in across R to the R of the R foot. Transfer weight to L foot. Both toes are facing the reverse line of direction, feet are crossed	3	quick
Step R backward and pivot one-half counterclockwise on the R foot	1	quick
Bring the L foot up to the instep of the R foot and with the L toe help balance on the R foot	2, 3	quick quick

Closed position, the lead facing the line of direction.

Starting L, the lead takes the step side cross while the follow, starting R, takes the back pivot }	1, 2, 3	all quick
Starting R, the lead takes the back pivot while the follow, starting L, takes step side across }	1, 2, 3	all quick

STYLE: The couple remains in closed position throughout. The steps are small as the follow is turning on a small pivot base while the lead takes step side cross. Since the lead turns one–quarter on his forward step, his second step is in the line of direction, a small step and cross on third beat. Then he steps back a short step and pivots while the follow takes the step side cross. The dancers always progress in the line of direction. Use two Waltz steps for one complete turn. The body resistance is firm for both lead and follow. They must lean away, pressing outward but keeping the center of gravity over the pivoting feet. The shoulders tilt slightly in one direction and then the other; tilt left as the left foot leads, right as the right foot leads. Do not resist the momentum of body weight, but rather give into the momentum.

LEAD: Firm body and arms in correct position. The momentum comes from the rapid transfer of the body forward in the line of direction every time on count 1.

CUE: 1, 2, 3, 1, 2, 3.

Viennese Step: The true Viennese with a step pivot repeated over and over is in closed dance position. Lead starting left forward, follow right backward.

STEPS	3/4 COUNTS	RHYTHM CUE
Step L forward, pivoting on the ball of the foot one-half counterclockwise; the right foot coming up to the instep of the L and with the R toe, helps to balance on the L foot	1, 2, 3	all quick
Step R backward, pivoting on the ball of the foot one-half counterclockwise; the L foot coming to the instep of the R helps to balance on the R foot	1, 2, 3	all quick

STEP CUE: Step pivot, step pivot.

STYLE: There is a lift of the body going into the pivot, which lifts the body weight, momentarily allowing the feet to pivot with less weight. Take care not to throw the weight off balance.

LEAD: Same as above.

VARIATIONS: The hesitation step as given under the box pattern is very helpful in giving a rest from the constant turning. Also, by using an uneven number of hesitation steps, the right foot is free and the whole Viennese turn may be changed to a clockwise turn starting with the right foot and applying the pattern with opposite footwork.

WALTZ COMBOS

These Waltz routines are combinations for practice, listed from simple to complex. (Closed position, unless otherwise indicated.)

1. *Balance and Box*
   2 balance steps (forward, backward)
   4 box steps
2. *Waltz Box*
   1 box step
   2 forward Waltz steps
   1 box turn
3. *Cross Box and Turn*
   2 cross steps
   1 box turn

4. *Hesitation and Box Turn*
   2 hesitation steps (forward, backward)
   1 box turn
5. *Cross Step and Weaving*
   2 cross steps
   1 weaving step
6. *Advanced Combo*
   1 box turn
   4 twinkle steps
   2 hesitation steps
   2 pursuit Waltz steps
   1 corté
   1 forward Waltz step

7. *Advanced Combo*
   6 streamline steps (18 beats)
   2 twinkle steps
   4 streamline steps
   2 hesitation steps

3

SWING (*Jitterbug*)

Swing IS AN UMBRELLA TERM for a wide variety of dance, such as West Coast Swing, East Coast Swing, Jive, Jitterbug, Shag, and Lindy Hop. With the advent of Dixieland jazz during the Roaring Twenties, a variety of dances appeared, including the *Lindbergh Hop*. Cab Calloway is credited with referring to the Lindy hoppers as "jitterbuggers." The dance went through a fad period of being extremely eccentric with its wild acrobatics inspired by the rising popularity of boogie woogie. The Big Apple, the Shag, and the Swing were all products of that period. They changed after World War II to a more syncopated rhythm called rock and roll with the Double Time Swing pattern and to the Swing with the smooth, sophisticated triple rhythm, which came in a short time later. All during the Rock period, both Double and Triple Time Swing could be seen on American Bandstand. A softer sound called boogie, but no relation to boogie woogie, has greater synthesization of electronic equipment.

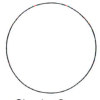

Circular Space
for
Swing Dance

Swing is danced to a wide variety of music and reflects the dance style of the particular music—Big Band music of the '40s, rock and roll, rhythm and blues, Salsa, Reggae, Country Western, and Cajun—all written in 4/4 or cut time. Swing includes the rhythm of Lindy Hop, Single Time, Double Time, and Triple Time. Some refer to these as Jitterbug. The term *Swing* is also applied to myriad of figures as the couple covers a *circular space* in one area. There is wide variation in the footwork and figures.

East Coast Swing and *Triple Time* are synonymous. *West Coast Swing* is a more difficult and sophisticated dance. West Coast Swing is referred to as a *slot dance* because the couple moves back and forth in a narrow space, always the same space. The dance evolved in the '50s on the West Coast in the small clubs where dance space was limited.

We will continue to use the term *Swing* for Single, Double, and Triple Time Swing; Circular Space for Swing Dance; and Narrow Space for West Coast Swing Dance.

SWING RHYTHM

Swing is written in 4/4 or cut time. It is extremely adaptable to fast or slow rhythm or to 4/4 time from Foxtrot to hard rock in quality. The Shag was actually the first dance to be called Jitterbug, and its slow slow quick quick rhythm set the pattern for all of the others. The Single Time Swing has the same rhythm.

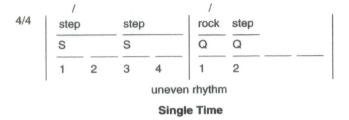

Single Time

Double Time is very adaptable to slow or fast music. This style was very popular in the '50s. Accent is on the offbeat.

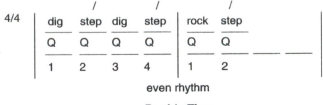

Double Time

Triple Time is more often danced to the slow, blues, sophisticated tempos.

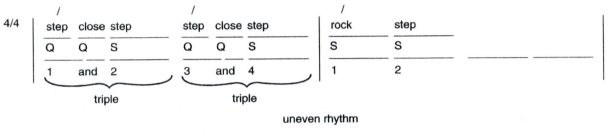

Triple Time—East Coast Swing

SWING STYLE

Exciting styles and positions are in use for Swing. It is a matter of taste for the individual dancers whether they use a dig step, a step–hop, or a kick step. However, the basic rhythm must be maintained by both lead and follow to coordinate the pattern together, unlike Discotheque (dancing apart), in which the step or rhythm pattern of each partner is unstructured. The lead is able to lead the dance because of the magnificent body alertness of both partners. A firm body and tone in the arm and fingers enable quick response in any direction. The space between partners is controlled by a spring tension in the elbow, which never extends fully but allows the pull away and the spring back to occur smoothly and with control. The follow uses her arm as a pivot center. The elbow is down and the hand is up for the underarm turns, and she turns around her arm but does not let it fly in the air. There should never be the appearance of arms flying loose or entangled. The fingers slip easily around one another without losing contact. Even the free arm is bent and remains close to the body.

Swing steps tend to cover a circular space in one area of the floor. The footwork is at all times small and close together, with rolling and turning on the ball of the foot. The turning action for beginner steps is always on the first step (count 2) of the pattern when the follow is on her right foot and the lead is on his left. The rhythm pattern is generally the same over and over but the changes of position and direction and the constant subtle smooth roll to offbeat rhythm generates a fabulous excitement for both dancer and observer.

Directions are for the lead; the follow's part is reversed, except when noted.

Single Time Swing— Side-to-Side Basic

(Beginners—two hands joined; experienced—Social Swing position)

STEPS	4/4 COUNTS	RHYTHM CUE	VERBAL CUE
Step L in place	1	slow	left
Step R in place	2	slow	right
Step L backward, a little behind R heel, using ball of L foot	3	quick	rock
Step R in place	+	quick	step

STEP CUE: Left, right, rock step or side, in place, rock step.

PARTNER CONNECTION: The dancers take two hands joined at approximately waist height, the lead's hands palm up. The elbow is down. The arms have tone in them and should not be limp. Fingers are together in a shape. Slightly angle fingers in partner's hands, so they do not dig into their palms. Exert a gentle pull against partner's fingers without squeezing! Lead's thumbs rest lightly on the follow's knuckles.

STYLE: The body takes a *slight* motion, leaning to the side from the waist and dipping the outside shoulder (lead's left, follow's right) on the first step. Take care not to exaggerate this motion. It is very subtle. The first step is a small step, approximately 12", or shoulder distance apart. Return to normal posture on the second step. Do not take the full body weight back on the rock step. On the rock step there is a spring tension in the arms that allows an apart–together action that is smooth and has arm control. The weight is carried on the balls of the feet and the steps are small throughout. There is a small amount of knee bend, depending on individual preference and style; however, the action should be smooth and not bouncy.

NOTE: Beginners should practice the foot pattern alone until they can move accurately with the rhythm. Then dancers take two hands and practice the foot work together.

LEAD: The lead lowers his left arm down (a reverse curl action), while slightly dipping his left shoulder on the first side step. On the second step, the lead returns his arms to the starting position in preparation for the rock step. Arm cue: Drop, Recover, Rock step.

The basic step is usually used to start dancing together and establish a connection with your partner. Once the connection is established, the lead begins to incorporate different variations, or steps. The following is a short list of swing dance steps.

The lead's hands must be able to rotate easily in the follow's hands during any variation.

Arch and Trade

Wrap (Cuddle)

Two Hands to Social Swing

Inside Turn (Underarm Turn)

Octopus

Basic in Social Swing

Walk Through (Brush Off)

Hammerlock

Arch Out from Semiopen

Tuck Spin

Turning Basic (Collegiate)

ARCH AND TRADE

(Two hands joined)

The lead lifts his left arm up (forming the "arch"), the follow goes under the arch, trading places.

STEPS	STEP CUE
Lead steps L forward while raising L arm up and slightly left	slow
Follow steps R forward	
Lead step R, turning 1/4 counterclockwise	slow
Follow, pivoting on R 180° clockwise, while turning under lead's arm, steps back L	
Lead, pivots 1/4 counterclockwise and rock steps	rock steps
Follow rock steps	
Finish move with an inside turn (see below).	

STEP CUE: Lift (lead's left arm), follow turn, rock step.

STYLE: Follow keeps right forearm at a right angle and right elbow at shoulder level. The follow turns around her own arm, not under it. Both take small steps, insuring that their arms have a slight bend in them for the rock step.

LEAD: As the lead lifts his arm up, he gives a gentle pull back, guiding the follow under his arm. The lead's left arm is up and slightly left of them, allowing the follow a clear path to go under his arm.

NOTE: The lead lifts his arm up high enough so that the follow does not need to duck to go under, but the lead only lifts his arm as high as the follow's head. Lifting the arm too high above the follow will tend to pull her arm above a comfortable level.

INSIDE TURN (UNDERARM TURN)

(Swing Out position)

The lead and follow exchange places as the lead turns the follow counterclockwise across to his position and steps around to the follow's position.

STEPS	STEP CUE
Lead steps L forward turning 1/4 clockwise, while raising L hand toward right shoulder, going over the follow's head	slow
Follow steps R forward turning 1/4 counterclockwise, moving under the lead's arm	
Lead continues to turn 1/4 clockwise, then steps back R, lowering L hand	slow
Follow continues turning counterclockwise and steps back L	
Both rock step. To perform a basic next, join both hands, or to repeat, stay in Swing Out position	rock step

STEP CUE: Lift (lead's left arm), follow turns, rock step.

STYLE: Both turn halfway around on the first step, staying close together. They have exactly exchanged places after one complete pattern.

LEAD: The lead turns his hand knuckles up, fingers down, so that the follow's fingers can slip around the lead's fingers.

NOTE: This underarm turn can be repeated over and over. It may serve as a connecting step to any other variation or can be used to return to the basic after ending in Swing Out position.

WALK THROUGH (BRUSH OFF)

(Swing Out position, or if starting from two hands joined, the lead must release his right hand.)

The lead and follow exchange places as the lead does a left turn while seemingly moving through his partner's arm.

STEPS	STEP CUE
Lead steps diagonally L forward on L foot while turning 1/4 counterclockwise	slow
The lead's left hand pulls down toward his right hip, guiding the follow behind him	
Follow steps forward right	
Lead steps side on R foot, releasing his L hand on R side and moving his L hand to L side,	slow
(palm facing back) to reconnect with follow's R hand	
Follow pivots 1/4 clockwise and steps side with L foot, lightly sliding R hand along	
partner's waist to reconnect with their left hand	
Lead pivots on R foot 1/4 counterclockwise to face partner and rock step	rock step
Follow pivots on L foot 1/4 clockwise to face partner and rock step	
Finish move with inside turn, page 64	

STEP CUE: Lead turns, reconnect, rock step.

STYLE: As the lead turns, his free right hand must reach over his left arm.

LEAD: The lead must turn his body sharply 1/4 counterclockwise, providing the follow a space to move through. If this turn is not done, the follow will bump into the lead's shoulder.

NOTE: At the end of this move, the lead's left hand will be palm facing down (or opposite of normal). Do not try and flip the hand. While performing the inside turn, the hands will automatically rotate to the normal position.

TUCK SPIN

(Two hands joined)

STEPS	STEP CUE
Lead steps in place while moving both of the follow's hands to lead's R side	slow
(follow turns slightly to her L)	
Lead steps R in place, pushing the follow in the opposite direction (releasing hands)	slow
with a quick flick, spinning the follow clockwise	
Follow does a full turn clockwise, spinning on both feet	
Rejoin hands for the rock step	rock step

STEP CUE: Tuck, spin, rock step.

STYLE: The follow must spin smoothly a full turn in place, standing tall, not losing her balance. Sliding the left foot to the right will facilitate spinning on both feet.

LEAD: The lead must give a firm, quick lead, allowing the follow to respond with the proper timing.

NOTE: The lead may also spin at the same time, moving counterclockwise.

WRAP (CUDDLE)

(Two hands joined)

STEPS	STEP CUE
Part I	
Lead steps L in place while lifting L arm, preparing to turn follow counterclockwise Follow step R foot forward and diagonally across L foot	slow
Lead steps R in place while moving left hand in a counterclockwise circle in front of partner's face and continuing around his head Follow pivots on R foot 180° counterclockwise and step back on L foot, finishing with follow on lead's R side; hands are at the follow's waist level	slow
Both rock step	rock step
Part II	
Lead steps forward on L foot while lifting L arm; a roll out is initiated with a gentle R forearm push on the follow's back Follow steps forward on R foot	slow
Lead steps back (in place) on R foot Follow pivots 180° clockwise on R foot stepping back on L foot	slow
Both rock step	rock step
The lead's L hand is slightly rotated after the follow rolls out; finishing this move with an inside turn, page 64, put the lead's hand in the upright position	

STEP CUE: Lift (lead's left arm), cuddle in, rock step, cuddle out, rock step.

STYLE: A smooth, continuous roll in (cuddle in) is important.

LEAD: The lead must lift his left hand and circle (wrap) it around the follow's head. It is important to let the hands (lead's left, follow's right) rotate easily while performing this move.

NOTE: Once a couple is in the cuddle position, it is an option to stay there for a few extra beats. Foot work for both lead and follow is forward, in place (back), rock step. Another variation on the cuddle out (unwrap) is for the lead to release with his left hand and pull gently with his right hand, rolling the follow out to the lead's right side.

OCTOPUS

(Two hands joined)

STEPS	STEP CUE
Part I	
Lead steps diagonally L forward on L foot Follow steps diagonally L forward on R foot, ending R hip to R hip	slow
Lead steps in place R while swinging both arms up and over both heads Both partners lower L hand behind their own head and R hand behind partner's head (Octopus position)	slow
Lead releases both hands and slides right hand along follow's right arm, catching R hands. Both partners turn 1/8 R to catch R hand and perform rock step	rock step
Part II *(turn follow and change hands behind the lead's back)*	
Lead raises R elbow and turns follow clockwise under R arm while stepping L foot diagonally across R foot Follow pivots 180° counterclockwise on L (turning under lead's arm) and steps back R	slow
Lead lowers R arm behind his back putting the follow's R hand into the lead's L hand while stepping side R with R foot Follow steps L foot back	slow

Lead pivots on R foot 90' counterclockwise, moving L hand from behind back to front and faces follow for rock step

Finish move with inside turn, page 64

STEP CUE: Up, and over, rock step.

Follow turns, change hands, rocks step.

LEAD: The lead must lift both hands high enough to go over both partner's heads, not just his own.

NOTE: Once the follow has the lead, she must let her arms float up and not pull down on the lead's arms.

HAMMERLOCK

(Two hands joined)

This is just like the arch and trade, continuing to hold on to both hands. The follow ends up with her left arm folded behind her back in a Hammerlock (wrestling term) position.

STEPS	STEP CUE
Lead steps forward L while raising L arm up and slightly left	slow
Lead's R hand moves to his L side, giving a gentle pull, guiding the follow forward	
Follow steps forward R, going under lead's left arm	
Lead steps R, turning 180° counterclockwise ending R hip to R hip, lowering left arm down in front of lead's body	slow
Follow, pivoting on R 180° clockwise while turning under lead's arm, steps back L	
Both rock step in hammerlock position	rock step
Using one full basic, reverse the pattern to return to two hands position	

STEP CUE: Lift (lead's left arm), turn (both lead and follow), rock step.

LEAD: As the lead lifts his arm up, he gives a gentle pull back, guiding the follow under his arm. To reverse the hammerlock, the leads give a *very gentle* pull with his right hand on the follow's left arm.

NOTE: On the reverse, the lead can spin the follow with his left hand (releasing the right hand) 1½ times back to two hands joined position. The spinning action is lead with the lead's wrist moving in a circular motion (counterclockwise), around the follow's head. The lead drops his arm back to waist height to stop the follow from spinning. The spin is done during the slow slow, rejoining both hands for the rock step.

TURNING BASIC (COLLEGIATE)

(Two hands joined)

During one basic, the couple will rotate 180°. This is an intermediate move.

STEPS	STEP CUE
Lead steps diagonal L forward	slow
Follow steps diagonal L forward with R foot, almost ending R hip to R hip	
Lead pivots on L foot 180° clockwise and crosses R foot behind left	slow
Follow pivots on R foot 90° clockwise, steps side left	
Lead faces partner for rock step	rock step
Follow pivots 90° clockwise on L to face partner for rock step	

STEP CUE: Side left, behind right (turn), rock step.

STYLE: This is a smooth, circular motion

LEAD: The lead must step strongly to diagonal left and drop left arm (reverse curl down) to give the follow the correct angle to step forward. The timing also must be sharp. If the lead is even a little late in leading this, the follow is already moving to the side.

VARIATIONS: A) An optional lead is to reach sideways with each hand shoulder high on the first step and bring the hands back together on the second step. This creates a butterfly turn effect. B) A second and more advanced option has the lead pivoting to right parallel position (right hip to right hip) on the first slow and to left parallel position (left hip to left hip) on the second slow.

TWO HANDS TO SOCIAL SWING

STEPS	STEP CUE
Lead and follow step toward each other, the lead pulling his L hand downward and placing R hand on follow's back, rib level	slow
Both step backward a short step in semiopen position	slow
Rock step in same position	rock step

STEP CUE: Pull down, come together, rock step.

STYLE: The steps are small.

LEAD: The lead pulls down on the follow's hand, guiding the follow into semiopen position.

BASIC IN SOCIAL SWING

(Social Swing position)

STEPS	STEP CUE
Lead steps L forward	slow
Lead steps R backward	slow
Rock step in place	rock step

STEP CUE: Forward, back, rock step.

STYLE: Dancers remain in social swing position throughout. All steps are small. The hand grasp is low with a straight elbow (not hyperextended), held in close to the body. The lead's fingers reach around the little–finger side of the follow's hand.

NOTE: This is a good rest step, or what is commonly used during a *Dance Jam.*

ARCH OUT FROM SEMIOPEN

(Social Swing position)

The lead takes the entire step pattern in place as he turns the follow out under his left arm to face him.

STEPS	STEP CUE
Lead steps L forward, lifting L arm up Follow steps R forward	slow
Lead steps in place R, giving the follow a gentle push on her back, turning her under the lead's L arm Follow pivots 180° on R foot (to face partner), stepping back with L foot	slow
Rock step in place	rock step

CUE: Lift, follow under, rock step

STYLE: Follow keeps right forearm at a right angle and right elbow at shoulder level. The follow turns around her own arm, not under it. Both take small steps, ensuring that their arms have a slight bend in them for the rock step.

LEAD: As the lead lifts his left arm up, he gives a gentle push with his right hand on the follow back, guiding the follow under his arm.

NOTE: The lead lifts his arm up high enough so that the follow does not need to duck to go under, but the lead only lifts his arm as high as the follow's head. Lifting the arm too high above the follow will tend to pull her arm above a comfortable level.

VARIATION: Instead of lifting the arm on the first slow, the lead can tuck (see tuck spin, page 65) the follow in on the first slow, then arching and spinning the follow under arm on the second slow.

Triple Time—East Coast Swing

TRIPLE TIME IS LOVELY AND pleasant to do to a nice swingy Foxtrot or blues song. It should be smooth and relaxing.

TRIPLE RHYTHM

(Social Swing position) (Three little steps to each slow beat; these are similar to a fast Two–Step.)

STEPS	4/4 COUNTS	RHYTHM CUE
Step L forward		
Close R to L, take weight R	1 *and* 2	quick quick slow
Step L forward		
Step R backward		
Close L to R, take weight L	3 *and* 4	quick quick slow
Step R backward		

STEP CUE: Triple step, triple step, rock step.

STYLE: The triple rhythm should be small shuffling steps, keeping the feet close to the floor. Weight is on the ball of the foot. Refer to basic swing style, page 62.

LEAD: The lead cues the follow for the triple steps by increasing the tension in his right hand as he starts the shuffle step forward.

VARIATIONS: Any of the variations for Double Time Swing can be done in triple rhythm, and dancers frequently change from one rhythm to another during one piece of music.

TRIPLE TIME SWIVEL STEP

(Social Swing position and traveling in line of direction, forward; rhythm pattern changes)

STEPS	4/4 COUNTS	RHYTHM CUE
Lead's Part (follow's part is the reverse)		
Step L forward		
Close R to L	1 *and* 2	quick quick slow
Step L forward		
Step R forward		
Close L to R	3 *and* 4	quick quick slow
Step R forward		
Pivot on R foot to face partner, and bring L foot alongside of it, shifting weight to L foot	1	slow
Pivot on L foot to face open position, bring R foot alongside of it, shifting weight to R foot	2	slow
Repeat pivot on R foot	3	slow
Repeat pivot on L foot	4	slow
Step L forward		
Close R to L	1 *and* 2	quick quick slow
Step L forward		
Step R backward		
Close L to R	3 *and* 4	quick quick slow
Step R backward		
(turning follow out clockwise in an underarm turn)		
Rock step (in swing out position)	1, 2	slow slow

STEP CUE: Triple step, triple step
swivel 2 3 4
triple step, triple step, rock step.

STYLE: The swivel steps are tiny, crisp, and neatly turning, just a quarter turn on each pivot. The body turns with the foot closed, open, closed, open.

LEAD: The lead must lead the swivel step by turning the follow from open to closed, and so forth.

NOTE: The couple progresses along the line of direction as the pivot turn is being done in four quick steps.

SWING COMBOS

The Swing routines are combinations for practice, which are listed from simple to complex. They may be used for either Single Time or Triple Time. (Two hands joined or social swing position, unless otherwise indicated.)

1. *Basic Swing Out and Close*
    1 basic
    single underarm break
    break to original position
2. *Basic–Swing Out–Underarm Turn Close*
    1 basic
    single underarm break
    break to original position
3. *Swing Out and Collegiate*
    2 basics
    single underarm break
    3 collegiate steps
    underarm turn
    original position

4. *Swing Out and Brush Off*
    2 basics
    single underarm break
    brush off
    underarm turn
    original position
5. *Collegiate–Brush Off*
    2 basic
    single underarm break
    underarm turn
    3 collegiate steps
    underarm turn
    brush off
    underarm turn
    original position

6. *Collegiate–Tuck–Spin*
    2 collegiate steps
    tuck spin
    underarm turn
7. *Collegiate–Wrap*
    2 collegiate steps
    wrap
    unwrap

8. *Wrap–Unwrap Spin*
    2 collegiate steps
    wrap
    unwrap
    tuck spin
    underarm turn

West Coast Swing

WEST COAST SWING RHYTHM

West Coast Swing Rhythm is 6 or 8 beats. It is a slower rhythm than East Coast Swing (120–130 BPM).

4/4	step	step	touch	step	anchor step step step step		
	S	S	S	S	Q	Q	S
	1	2	3	4	1	&	2
	1	2	3	4	5	&	6

triple

uneven rhythm—6 count

4/4	step	step	step step step			anchor step step step step		
	S	S	Q	Q	S	Q	Q	S
	1	2	3	&	4	1	&	2
	1	2	3	&	4	5	&	6

double   triple   triple

uneven rhythm—6 count

4/4	step	step	step step step			step	step	anchor step step step step		
	S	S	Q	Q	S	S	S	Q	Q	S
	1	2	3	&	4	1	2	3	&	4
	1	2	3	&	4	5	6	7	&	8

double   triple   double   triple

uneven rhythm—8 count

West Coast Swing is referred to as a slot dance because the couple moves back and forth repeatedly in the same narrow space. The dance evolved in the 50s on the West Coast in small clubs where dance space was limited.

The follow's step is different from the lead's; partners do not mirror each other. The step is like the Cuban walk (p. 116). Little kicks and toe touches on the beat give flair for a sophisticated look. The anchor steps (quick, quick, slow) occur at the end of the slot.

SUGAR PUSH

(Basic Step) (Two hands joined)

Anchor Step •

Anchor Step •

Narrow Space
for
West Coast Swing Dance

STEPS	COUNTS	STEP CUE
Lead's Part		
Step back L	1	step
Step R to L	2	together
Touch L	3	touch
Step forward L	4	step
Step R behind L (hook) in place and release lead's R, follow's L hand (swing out position)	5	hook
Step L in place, pushing off	*and*	step
Step R in place	6	step
Follow's Part		
Step forward R	1	step
Step forward L	2	step
Touch R to L instep	3	touch
Turning R towards partner, step back R (continue to travel in slot)	4	step
Step L behind R (hook) and release follow's L lead's R hand	5	hook
Step R in place	*and*	step
Step L in place	6	step

STEP CUE: The cue "walk" may be used for counts 1, 2, 4.

STYLE: The footwork and hips are like the Cuban walk (p. 116). Dig, pressing the foot into the floor while moving forward.

LEAD: The arms need to be firm (give weight) as the follow moves forward, the lead pulling toward himself. On count 3 the follow leans a little more forward, body rising to receive the *push*. On count 4 the lead *pushes* as the follow moves backward. Both dancers must offer resistance. The lead initiates the *pull* and *push*.

NOTE: The steps on counts 5 and 6 are the "anchor steps." The follow may choose to do a "coaster step" for counts 5 and 6. Coaster step is step back left, close right to left, step forward left.

VARIATION: Triple step. Counts 3 4 become "3 and 4" (QQS). Instead of Touch Step, lead steps left right left, follow steps right left right.

UNDERARM TURN

(Swing Out position)

The follow passes the lead's right side, turns under her arm to face opposite direction.

STEPS	COUNTS	STEP CUE
Lead's Part		
Moving to L side, step L	1	step
Step forward R	2	step
Moving toward slot, step L, pivoting clockwise	3	side
Step R, still turning	*and*	step
Raising L arm, step L into the slot (now facing opposite direction)	4	step
Step R behind L	5	hook
Step L	*and*	step
Step R in place	6	step
Follow's Part		
Step forward R	1	step
Step forward L	2	step
Take 3 running steps (R, L, R) to the end of slot, turning counterclockwise under R arm, on count 4	3 *and* 4	run, run, turn
Step L behind R	5	hook
Step R	*and*	step
Step L in place	6	step

LEAD: Lead pulls the follow forward, left hand down, raises arm for turn on count 4.

NOTE: Alternate one Sugar Push sequence with one Underarm Turn. Follow may use "coaster step" for counts 5 and 6.

LEFT SIDE PASS

(Swing Out position)

Follow passes lead's left side.

STEPS	COUNTS	STEP CUE
Lead's Part		
Moving to R side, step L across R	1	step
Pivoting counterclockwise on L, step R near L (now facing slot)	2	step
Following the follow, take 3 steps (L, R, L)	3 *and* 4	step, step, step
Facing opposite direction, step R behind L	5	hook
Step L	*and*	step
Step R in place	6	step
Follow's Part		
Step forward R	1	step
Step forward L	2	step
Passing partner (lead's left side), traveling in the slot, take 3 short running steps (R, L, R) pivoting counterclockwise on last run	3 *and* 4	run, run, turn
Facing opposite direction, step L behind R	5	hook
Step R	*and*	step
Step L	6	step

NOTE: The Left Side Pass is usually preceded by one Sugar Push.

STYLE: The follow holds left arm, elbow bent, to chest as she passes partner and turns.

LEAD: On count 4 lead drops left shoulder, pulls his left hand down as follow passes.

WHIP

(Swing Out position)

Starting in Swing Out position, couple moves into closed position, makes one complete turn clockwise as a couple at the center of the slot, separates into Swing Out position, and ends in original position.

STEPS	COUNTS	STEP CUE
Lead's Part		
Step back L	1	step
Moving to L side, step R across L and move into closed position	2	cross
Step L forward, pivoting clockwise as a couple	3	turn
Continuing to turn, step R in place	*and*	and
Step L across slot (L and R feet straddle slot)	4	step
Step R behind L (hook), continuing to turn as a couple	5	hook
Releasing lead's R, follow's L hand and separating, step L forward into slot. Now facing original direction	6	step
Step R behind L, step L, step R in place	7 *and* 8	hook, step, step
Follow's Part		
Step forward R toward partner	1	step
Moving into closed position step L pivoting clockwise to face partner	2	pivot
Step back R	3	back
Close L to R	*and*	together
Step R forward between the lead's two feet	4	step
Continuing to turn clockwise as a couple, step L	5	step
Release follow's L, lead's R hand and step back R	6	step
Step L behind R, step R, step L in place	7 *and* 8	hook, step, step

NOTE: Follow's Part, counts 3 and 4, is a *coaster step*. It may be cued as "coaster step" (3 *and* 4) (QQS).

Lindy Hop

THE *LINDY HOP* EMERGED IN the late 1920s to a sound of a new style of music being played in Harlem. The African American jazz musicians of that day called this new rhythm "swinging the beat" (Wagner 1997, p. 8). The music was swinging and so were the dancers. The name *Lindy Hop* came from a dancer named Shorty Snowden. During a dance marathon in the '20s, a reporter asked him what he was doing, and in honor of Charles Lindbergh's recent "hop" over the Atlantic, he said, "Lindy Hop." The Lindy Hop is considered the granddaddy of all the American swing forms.

The Lindy Hop incorporated many moves from a previous dance fad, the Charleston. Many other steps, often theatrical, were created for dance contests in Harlem. An example is *Air Steps*, or putting the women in the air with a flip.

The Lindy Hop's popularity was driven by many events of the day. Whitey's Lindy Hopper, a dance troupe from Harlem, toured the United States and Europe. Popular movies, such as *Day at the Races* and *Hellzapoppin*, included Lindy Hop dance scenes. These factors helped the Lindy Hop continue to gain popularity as it moved into middle class America. A *Life* magazine article in 1943, marking a high point of popularity, called the Lindy Hop "America's true Folk Dance." After World War II, the Lindy Hop's popularity declined.

In the Mid '80s, dancers from California (Erin Stevens and Steve Mitchell), Sweden (founding members of the Rhythm Hot Shots), and England (the Jiving Lindy Hoppers) went to New York seeking the guidance of some original Lindy Hoppers. These people wanted to learn more than what they had seen in old movies or magazines (Erin Stevens, personal communication). Frankie Manning, an original member of Whitey's Lindy Hoppers, had just started dancing again, after retiring from the post office. These dancers worked with Frankie and other original Lindy Hop dancers and used this new knowledge to revive the Lindy Hop.

More recently, the Lindy Hop has exploded onto the dance scene. Movies like *Swing Kids* and *Malcolm X* have Lindy Hop dance sequences. TV commercials are using the Lindy Hop (the most notable is the spring 1998 Gap Khaki "Swings" ad campaign). Bands are playing music in the style of the '30s and '40s swing bands (Big Bad Voodoo Daddy). The Lindy Hop revival is in full swing!

STYLE: Knees are bent and there is a constant gentle bounce throughout the movements. Bend over slightly from the waist. Follows are slightly more upright than the leads. Self–expression is encouraged.

MUSIC: Normal tempo is 140–160 BPM.

FULL LINDY BASIC

(Swing Out–Lindy position)

Starting in Swing Out–Lindy position, couple moves into closed position, makes one complete turn clockwise as a couple, and separates into Swing Out position.

STEPS	COUNTS	STEP CUE
Lead's Part		
Step back L, bending slightly forward, look at partner. Leave R foot in place	1	rock
Step in place R	2	step
Pivoting one-quarter clockwise, step forward L	3	three
Right hand moves to social position		
Pivoting one-eighth clockwise step R behind left (leave left foot in place)	*and*	and
Pivoting one-eighth clockwise step left in place, left knee bent	4	four
Face Off Position		
Step R behind L (hook) in place, release right hand	5	hook
Pivoting one-quarter clockwise on R, step side L on L	6	step
Pivoting one-quarter clockwise on L, step back R	7	step
Step L in place	*and*	in
Step R in place	8	place

Follow's Part

Step	Count	
Step swivel R, wave left hand in the air	1	swivel
Step swivel L, wave left hand in the air	2	swivel
Step forward R	3	three
Pivoting one-quarter clockwise, step side L with L (leave right foot in place)	and	and
Pivoting one-quarter clockwise, step R in place	4	four
Face Off Position		
Pivoting one-quarter clockwise, step side L	5	run
Remove left hand from lead's shoulder		
Step side L with R, crossing R in front	6	run
Step side L with L	7	step
Pivoting one-quarter clockwise, step R in place	and	in
Step L in place	8	place

STYLE: Always keep eye contact with partner. On counts 1 and 2, the lead is mimicking "bowing down" to the follow. On Counts 1 and 2 the follow may vary her arm movement.

LEAD: On count "3 *and*," lead leans forward with left shoulder. The lead releases right hand on count 5, allowing the follow to move away.

VARIATIONS: On counts 1 and 2, either the lead or the follow may change their footwork: for example, a heel drop or a kick away may be substituted. These variations are executed independent of the partner.

BASIC TO A JOCKEY

(Swing Out–Lindy position)

Starting in Swing Out–Lindy position, lead makes one complete turn clockwise (follow, one and a half), bringing the follow to his right side, ending in the Jockey position.

STEPS	COUNTS
Repeat count 1–4 for Full Lindy Basic	

Lead's Part

Step	Count
Step in place R. Do not release right arm as in the basic, with right arm, reach around to partner's right side, starting to bring her into the Jockey position.	5
Pivoting one-half clockwise on R, Step side L	6
Step back R	7
Step L in place (next to R)	and
Step back R	8

Follow's Part

Step	Count
Pivoting one-quarter clockwise on R, step side L	5
Pivoting one-quarter clockwise on L, step forward R	6
Pivoting one-quarter clockwise on R, step side L	7
Step R in place (next to L)	and
Pivoting one-quarter clockwise on R, step back L	8

LINDY CHARLESTON

(Jockey position)

Directions are for the lead. The follow's footwork is reversed.

STEPS	COUNTS	STEP CUE
Step back L	1	rock
Step in place R	2	step
Kick L forward	3	kick
Step L	4	step
Kick R forward	5	kick
Swing R foot back to place	6	and
Kick R back	7	kick
Step R	8	step

NOTE: This step is usually repeated two to three times.

STYLE: Lead releases his left hand, follow's right hand. Free arms swing forward and back during the Charleston footwork. A constant bounce is maintained during the step.

JOCKEY TO A SWING OUT

STEPS	COUNTS	STEP CUE
Lead's Part		
Repeats the footwork of Lindy Basic	1–8	
Follow's Part		
Step back R	1	rock
Step in L	2	step
Step R forward	3	step
Step L together	and	together
Step R forward (now in face off position)	4	step
Repeat count 5–8 of Lindy Basic, ending in Swing Out–Lindy position	5–8	

LEAD: Lead rejoins his left hand with follow's right hand on counts 7 and 8 of the previous measure. By count 4, the lead's right hand has returned to the middle of the follow's back.

SHINE

(Swing Out–Lindy position)

The lead stays in place, bringing his knees together and apart as the follow swivel steps clockwise around him, waving her left hand in the air; this is *Shining*.

STEPS	COUNTS	STEP CUE
Lead's Part (wobbly knees)		
With feet together, weight on L, both knees go to the side	*and*	and
Step in place R and bring knees together	1	in
Both knees go to the side	*and*	and
Step in place L and bring knees together	2	in
Repeat counts: *and* 1 *and* 2	*and* 3–8	
Repeat count 1–8		

Follow's Part

Starting with R, follow takes 16 swivel steps to move clockwise around the lead

STYLE: The follow is trying to attract attention, waving and smiling as she moves around the lead.

LEAD: On approximately count 5 of a basic, the lead would say "Hey Baby, do you want to Shine?" During the next basic he waits for a yes or no answer from the follow. When he hears a "yes," at the end of that basic, the shine starts. He continues to hold on to the follow's right hand with his left as she moves around him.

4

COUNTRY WESTERN

COUNTRY WESTERN DANCE has been around for a long time; it is definitely a grassroots dance. As country western music has increased in popularity so has Country Western Dance. Country western music, a twangy honky–tonk sound as played by Bob Wills and his Texas Playboys in the late 1930s, was just the beginning. The music is influenced by spirituals, Dixieland jazz, and the big band sound. The fiddle, steel guitar, and deep bass give country western music its character. The fiddle was part of the band. Wherever country western music is played, people dance. The dances are based on old Folk Dances, Square Dances, and Social Dances, topped off with a new look, called Country Western. *Swing, One-Step, Two-Step, Schottische, Waltz,* and *Line Dances* are all part of the repertoire.

COUNTRY WESTERN STYLE

The Country Western look starts with cowboy or roper boots. Tight fitting jeans are worn by both men and women. Large belt buckles adorn the dancers. Cowboy hats are commonly seen on the dance floor, though, for the last few years, younger men have been switching to baseball hats. In some settings, women may wear a western skirt instead of jeans. When dancers have a free hand, they hook the thumb near the belt buckle or into the closest pocket.

DANCE HALL ETIQUETTE

At Country Western Dances, several types of dancing may take place simultaneously. The perimeter of the dance floor is for round dances; the slower ones dance in the inside lane. Fast and slow dancers move counterclockwise around the floor. The Swing Dancers and Line Dancers split the center area, with line dancers closer to the band.

The lead takes the follow's hand or arm or offers his arm to escort her onto or off the dance floor and to return her to her seat.

In Western and Cajun dancing it is customary to leave the dance floor and return to your table or side of the room, even if you plan to dance the next dance with the same partner. The lead still takes the follow's hand or arm and offers his arm to escort her onto and off the dance floor and to return her to her seat.

Traditional Country Western Swing

TRADITIONAL COUNTRY WESTERN SWING RHYTHM

Traditional Country Western Swing is danced to a faster 4/4 time song, between 170 and 200 BPM. At times the traditional "cowboys" dance faster than the music, dancing with the music, not to the beat of the music. On popular country music TV programs and at many dance studios, the style of country swing performed is the East Coast Swing. The only difference from ballroom style is the music played.

COWBOY SWING STYLE

The cowboys have a very smooth style. They slide their feet along the floor, almost never picking them up for a step. The emphasis of the dance is on the arm movements and the figures that are performed more so than the footwork. During many figures, the feet may not move at all.

Steps are small and arms are kept bent and close to the body. Two factors figured in the development of this style: (1) the fast tempo of music does not allow for large ges–tures, and (2) traditional dance floors were very small. Large steps or movement would cause a couple to bump into another couple.

Although from a distance, this style may look wild, with a good partner, the moves are very controlled and flow smoothly from one variation to another. There is a con–stant counterbalance between partners, allowing a "leaning" away (with a bend at the elbow joint) that is the characteristic mark of Cowboy Swing.

BASIC STEP

(Two hands joined)

STEPS	4/4 COUNTS	RHYTHM CUE
Step L, diagonal L forward	1 *and*	slow
Follow: Step R, diagonal L forward (crossing in front of her L foot)		
Step R forward	2 *and*	slow
Pivot 180° counterclockwise on R foot	3	quick
Slide L to R foot, *keep weight on R foot*	*and*	quick
Begin again	4	

The Basic must be done four times to start at the beginning of the next measure.

STEP CUE: One, Two, Together.

STYLE: The Basic Step is performed moving in a counterclockwise motion. Knees slightly bent and forearms at the side with elbows bent. The lead and follow lean away from each other (counterbalance). Letting go would cause a partner to fall backwards. Shoulders are slightly back and hips are over the heels. On the *together* step of the Basic, some cowboys will touch their left foot to the side or slightly lift it off the floor for a little extra flair.

LEAD: On count *1 and*, the lead pulls the left side of his body back, guiding his partner to his right side. On count 3, the lead brings both hands in front of him for a counterbalance with his partner.

COWBOY SWING VARIATIONS

The lead's hands must be able to rotate easily in follow's hands during any variation.

Cowboy Arch	Cowboy Cuddle	Octopus
Cowboy Cross	Walk Through (Brush Off)	Pretzel

COWBOY ARCH

(Two hands joined)

The lead lifts up his left arm (forming the "arch") and goes under as follow goes behind him, trading places. Prep: Lead releases his right hand.

STEPS	STEP CUE
Lead steps diagonally left forward on L while raising L arm	one
Lead steps R forward while turning one-quarter L (L shoulder back)	two
Lead lowers L arm and leans back over R foot, counterbalancing with his partner in a swing out position	together
Finish move with follow's inside turn, page 64	

STEP CUE: Lead, Goes, Under.

STYLE: As the lead goes under his arm, he bends his knees so that he does not knock off his hat.

In the swing out position, the lead is not facing his partner, but looks at her with his peripheral vision. "Real cowboys" look at their partners out of the corner of their eye.

LEAD: The lead's left hand guides follow to his right side.

COWBOY CROSS

(Two hands joined)

The lead lifts up both hands. Keeping them together, he leads the follow to his right side going under his hands, ending with arms in a "crossed" position.

STEPS	STEP CUE
Cross	
Lead steps forward on L while raising both hands	one
Lead moves over his L foot and turns one-quarter R (R shoulder back) while taking both hands over the follow's head	two
Follow on R foot pivots counterclockwise one-half turn	
Lead lowers both hands and leans back over L foot, counterbalancing with partner	together
Uncross (feet do not move)	
Lead lifts both hands up, brings follow in front of him, turning her clockwise	one
Lead lowers both hands to belt level and leans over his R foot, counterbalancing with partner	two
Lead repeats cross and uncross	
Finish move with follow's inside turn, page 64	

STEP CUE: Cross, Follow, Under.
Uncross, Cross, Uncross, Turn through.

STYLE: After the first step is taken, both the lead's and follow's feet remain in place, pivoting on both feet to face toward partner. Both lead and follow must keep their elbows bent on all counterbalances.

LEAD: Lead lifts both hands up and together and gently pulls the follow toward his right side to the cross position. The follow must allow the lead's hand to twist in hers, as she goes under his hands.

COWBOY CUDDLE

(Two hands joined)

STEPS	STEP CUE
Cuddle In	
Lead steps forward on L while raising his L hand	one
Without releasing hands, the lead will move his raised L hand across in front of her and up over her head as she is turning counterclockwise one-half on her R foot	two
Lead lowers L hand as the follow finishes in the cuddle position close to him on his R side. Lead leans forward over L foot, counterbalancing with his partner as she leans back over her L foot	together
Cuddle Out (feet do not move)	
Lead lifts L hand up and gently pushes with his R forearm against her back to start her turning clockwise one-half	one
Lead lowers L hands to belt level and leans back over his R foot, counterbalancing with partner	two
Lead repeats Cuddle In and Cuddle Out	
Finish move with follow's inside turn, page 64	

STEP CUE: Cuddle, In Cuddle, Out Cuddle, In Cuddle, Out Cuddle, Through.

STYLE: After the first step is taken, both lead's and follow's feet remain in place. The follow pivots on her feet to turn. Both lead and follow must keep their elbows bent on the Cuddle Out counterbalance.

LEAD: Lead lifts left hand up and gently pulls the follow toward his right. The follow must allow the lead's hand to twist in hers, as she goes under his hands. In the Cuddle position, the lead must be sure that his hands are at her waist level.

WALK THROUGH (BRUSH OFF)

(Two hands joined)

PREP: Let go of your right hand.

The lead moves through the space where the follow's left arm is, seemingly walking through the arm.

STEPS	STEP CUE
Lead steps diagonally left forward on L foot while turning counterclockwise (L shoulder back)	one
Lead continues to turn and steps side on R foot. Release L hand when it is pulled against R side	two
Lead leans back over R foot. Bring L hand to L side (palm facing back) to catch follow's R hand	together
Follow leans back over L foot and slides R hand along his waist to reconnect with his L hand (follow's palm up)	
Finish move with follow's inside turn, page 64	

STYLE: This move is often used at the end of a combination or to finish off a variation that has ended in the swing out position.

LEAD: Lead using left hand, pulls partner forward toward right side.

OCTOPUS

(Two hands joined)

STEPS	STEP CUE
Part I	
Lead steps diagonally L forward on L foot	one
Follow steps diagonally L forward on R foot, ending R hip to R hip	
Lead swings both arms up and over both heads; lowering L hand behind your head and your R hand behind your partner's head (Octopus position)	two
Lead lets go with both hands, and R hands slide along partner's right arm	together
Turn one-eighth to R and lean away catching R hands (keep R elbow bent)	
Part II	
Lead raises R elbow and pulls partner to R side; follow steps side R on R	one
Lead turns follow L (clockwise) under R arm; lead turns one-quarter counterclockwise (L shoulder back) (follow is behind lead) and step side R on your R; he folds R arm behind his back and brings L hand to L side	two
Lead puts her R hand into his L hand (behind his back); continue turning one-quarter clockwise (right shoulder back); lead leans back over R foot; Follow leans back over L foot; lead's L hand is holding follow's R hand	together
Finish move with follow's inside turn, page 64	

STEP CUE: Up and Over
       Change Hands
       Turn the follow

LEAD: Pull your partner to your right side by raising both arms.

PRETZEL

(Two hands joined; the lead's hands must be able to rotate easily in follow's hands.)

The lead moves through three different positions in one continuous move.

STEPS	STEP CUE
Part I: Lead's Hammerlock	
Lead steps diagonally L forward on L foot while raising left arm	one
Lead steps forward on R foot while turning clockwise one-quarter (L shoulder back) and goes under L arm (lead must lower L elbow so he does not hit partner in the face); lead folds R forearm to back in a hammerlock position	two
Lead pivots on both feet, continuing turning clockwise; extend L arm to L and in front of follow's waist	together
Follow steps back onto R foot while turning clockwise one-quarter	

Part II: Back to Back

Lead raises L arm; pulling follow behind him with R arm while stepping L on L foot to a slightly wider stance	one
Lead continues pulling partner to R. While passing back to back lead raises R arm and lowers L arm	two
Partners are now R hip to R hip, with L arms behind the back	together

Part III: Lead turns, pulls partner from behind

Lead bends right elbow 90°	one
Follow turns clockwise one-eighth while moving over R foot	
Lead pivots on both feet counterclockwise one-quarter (L shoulder back); at the same time lead brings R forearm over his head and lowers it to chest level, keeping L hand behind; follow is behind lead	two
Follow steps on L foot by lead's L side while turning clockwise one-quarter	
Lead releases his R hand while pulling L hand and partner from behind his back; lead raises L arm to pull partner under his arm and in front of him	together
Follow steps forward on R foot while passing under partner's arm; she pivots counterclockwise one-half (L shoulder back) and steps back on L foot	
End in swing out position	

Finish move with follow's inside turn, page 64

STEP CUE:
Lead,	Goes,	Under
Back	To,	Back
Over Lead's Head,		Pull Follow From Behind

STYLE: This move must flow from one part to the next effortlessly. Once the lead begins the Pretzel he does very little, if any, stepping. The follow must move around him as needed. This step is usually performed very quickly. Total control must be achieved before speed is increased.

LEAD: In Part I, the lead pulls right hand (palm facing back) back and down guiding the follow to right side. The lead continues to pull gently with right hand to turn follow's left shoulder to lead's left shoulder.

Texas Two-Step Swing

(Two hands joined)

Directions are for the lead; the follow's part is reversed.

STEPS	4/4 COUNTS	STEP CUE
Step L in place	1	step
Touch R to L	2	touch
Step R in place	3	step
Touch L to R	4	touch
Step L backward, a little behind R heel	1	rock
Step R forward	2	step

FIGURES: Swing Out position. The variations occur on the first 4 counts.

1. Follow turns clockwise under her right arm, in place.
2. Lead turns clockwise under his left arm in place.
3. Lead and follow exchange places as he turns her counterclockwise across to his position and steps around her to her position.
4. Two hands joined. The lead raises left arm, follow steps right toward partner, turning counterclockwise under his arm, steps left as she is side by side on his right. Lower lead's left and follow's right arms. Now in Cuddle position (Wrap). Rock, step. In this position, dancers may go forward, travel clockwise or counterclockwise in place dancing the Texas Two–Step. To unwrap, the lead initiates a reverse roll, turning the follow clockwise back to starting position.

Traditional Two-Step

THE *TRADITIONAL TWO-STEP* is also known as the *Shuffle*. The dance is done in a smooth, flowing style. The rhythm—slow, slow, quick, quick, exactly like the Fox Trot Magic rhythm—is known as a *shuffle* beat.

Different Two–Step rhythms, noteworthy for their many regional variations, exist. The Texas Two–Step is an example. Although most common in Texas, this dance is popular throughout the United States and Canada. Texas Two–Step rhythm is quick, quick, slow, or step–together step. The Traditional Two–Step is normally danced to music between 75 and 95 BPM. The Texas Two–Step may be danced to faster music, up to 120 BPM.

In the mid 1990s, Country Western dance competitions became popular. A modern style Two–Step, used for competitions, has a reversed rhythm; quick quick, slow, slow. This style is favored in urban dance studios. Beginning variations on the first "quick" creates a snappier look. In rural areas of the country, where dance is considered a social activity, the traditional rhythm is maintained.

TWO-STEP RHYTHM

The music is written in 4/4 time. The step pattern takes a measure and a half of music. It is an uneven rhythm pattern—slow, slow, quick quick.

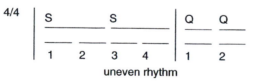

uneven rhythm

TWO-STEP STYLE

The dance has smooth, controlled steps; there is no pumping of arms or bouncing. The closed dance position has several variations. The body has good posture alignment, with a straight back and knees slightly bent. Quite a bit of space should be left between partners in variations of the closed position. The lead's left palm faces up and the follow's right palm faces down, resting lightly in lead's left; lead's right arm may be straight, right hand folding over follow's left shoulder. The position of the follow's left arm varies. The follow may fold her left hand over his right elbow; her elbow is down, her arm is limp, which gives a "careless look." Her left arm may be extended to rest on top of lead's right arm. Or she may hook her thumb into one of the lead's belt loops on his right side. They face each other squarely, shoulders parallel.

The dancers glide around the floor in a counterclockwise direction and cover a lot of territory. Although there are many variations, most dancers relax and move forward, with an occasional turn, or the lead dances backward, but always they move in the line of direction.

MUSIC: Suggested tune, "Mercury Blue."

(Closed position)

Directions are for the lead; the follow's part is reversed.

STEPS	4/4 COUNTS	RHYTHM CUE
Step L forward	1–2	slow
Step R forward	3–4	slow
Step L forward	1	quick
Step R forward	2	quick

STYLE: The forward steps should be long, smooth, gliding steps, straight ahead. The follow moving backward, takes a long step, reaching from hip to toe. If the music is slow, for balance on the slow steps, dancers may step forward left, touch right to left (for balance), step forward right, touch left to right.

LEAD: The body leads forward.

■ *Variations*

Over the past several years, many different variations have been added to the Two–Step repertoire. Some couples appear to be *swinging* as they move around the dance floor.

The basic footwork is maintained while executing the variations, which usually start on the first *slow*. Hands stay joined, except when noted. The lead's hands must always be able to rotate easily in the follow's hands. Once in position, the lead may decide to travel for a few Basics before moving on to the next position.

VARSOUVIENNE

(Starting from Closed position)

STEPS	CUES
Lead lifts L hand up and begins to turn follow counterclockwise 180°	S
Lead changes her R hand to his R hand continuing turning the follow 180°	S
Lead steps to follow's L side continuing turning her 180° (during the SSQQ the woman has turned one and one half times)	QQ
Lead shakes L hands with the follow ending in Varsouvienne position	
Lead lifts L hand and pulls down with R, causing the follow to turn clockwise 180°	S
Lead guides follow behind him	S
Lead lowers his L hand in front of follow. She steps up to his L side into a reverse Varsouvienne	QQ
Lead guides follow in front of him with L hand, starting to turn her clockwise 180°	S
Lead releases L hand and continues turning follow with his right hand 180°	S
Lead changes her R hand to his L, turning her 180° back to social position	QQ

LITTLE WINDOWS

(Starting from Varsouvienne position)

STEPS	CUES
Keeping R hand high, lead raises L hand over follow's head, turning her clockwise 180°	S
Lead continues turning follow clockwise 180° with both hands	S
Bring R arm to a 90° angle, lead finishes turning follow clockwise 180°, ending in Little Windows; R hips together, lead facing line of direction, follow facing reverse line of direction	QQ
This position may be reversed by turning the follow counterclockwise two and a half times, until the left hips are together, lead facing reverse line of direction and follow facing line of direction	
Return to closed position by turning the follow clockwise one and one-half turns	

YOKE

(Starting from Varsouvienne position)

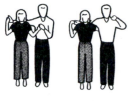

STEPS	CUES
Lead lifts his L hand up and over follow's head, gently turning her clockwise 180°	S
Keeping L hand high, lead moves R hand clockwise over follow's head, continuing turning her 180°	S
Lead lowers both hands behind necks, into a yoke position	QQ
This position may be reversed by turning the follow counterclockwise two turns in front of the lead, guiding her to his left side	
Return to closed position by turning the follow clockwise two turns	

Ten-Step

TEN–STEP IS ALSO known as the *Ten-Step Polka*. A similar dance, 8 beats, is the Jessie Polka. Country western dancers call the Jessie Polka the *Eight-Step Shuffle*, or *Cowboy Polka*.

METER: 2/4 fast or 4/4 slow. Directions are presented in beats.

RECORD: Grenn 25371.

MUSIC: Fiddle music; suggested tunes: "Uncle Pen," "Cajun Moon," "New Cut Road," "On the Road Again," "East Bound and Down."

STYLE: Review Line Dance style, page 92. Knees are slightly bent, keep the dance smooth.

POSITION: Couples in Varsouvienne position; follow's right-hand fingertips touch lead's right for ease of turn; lead's left hand reaches over (fingers down) follow's left, holding just above waist.

Part I

1–2	Beginning left—right knee bent—touch left heel forward, left foot turned to a 45° angle, and return; shift weight to left
3	Touch right toe backward
4	Brush (scuff) right heel as returning (no weight)
5	Touch right heel forward, right foot turned to a 45° angle
6	Sweep right, heel leading, across in front of left
7–8	Touch right heel forward, right foot turned to a 45° angle, and return, taking weight
9	Touch left heel forward, left foot turned to a 45° angle
10	Sweep left, heel leading, across in front of right

Part II

11–18	Beginning left, take four Two-Steps forward in line of direction (quick, quick, slow—four times)

VARIATIONS FOR PART II: Part I is referred to as "think steps" because the leader decides what variation to do. During Part II partners may improvise with a wide variety of maneuvers. The number of Two-Steps may be increased by an even number.

1. The follow turns under lead's left arm once or twice while moving forward.
2. Lead lifts right hand over follow's head, follow taking four Two-Steps turns toward the lead, and moves to his left side to face line of direction in promenade position. Repeat Part II; then lead raises his right arm over his head like a lariat and follow taking four Two-Steps travels behind the lead. She starts to turn counterclockwise 360° (third Two-Step); her right shoulder comes to his right shoulder; lead lifts his left arm up and extends his right arm down at his side, shoulder to shoulder; she pivots to face forward in original position (fourth Two-Step).
3. *The Train.* Taking four Two-Steps, follow moves in front of lead, two hands still joined and resting on her shoulders. Repeat Part II in this position. The follow Two-Steps back to place.
4. Take two Two-Steps forward; on the next two Two-Steps, the lead raises his right arm over her head, and the follow travels in front of lead to face him. Arms are crossed, extended and firm, with right hand on top. Repeat Part II. Pivoting counterclockwise, take four Two-Steps. Repeat Part II. The lead lifts right arm over his head as she travels around behind him, turning 360° as in variation 2 to face original position.
5. *Wheel Around.* In Varsouvienne position, take four Two-Steps; the couple turns counterclockwise, the lead dancing almost in place as the follow travels forward. Or turn clockwise, the follow dancing almost in place, as the lead travels forward.

Traveling Cha Cha

METER: 4/4 Directions are printed in beats.

BEATS:

1	2	3	&	4
Slow,	Slow,	Quick,	Quick,	Slow

MUSIC: "I Like It, I Love It" by Tim McGraw, "Big Heart" by The Gibson Miller Band, "I'm Not Strong Enough to Say No" by Blackhawk.

(Varsouvienne position)

BEATS	STEPS
1–2	Beginning left, rock forward and backward right
3 & 4	Cha cha cha; shuffle backward left, right, left
5–6	Rock backward right, rock forward left
7 & 8	Cha cha cha; shuffle forward right, left, right
1–4	Repeat action of beats 1–4 above
5–8	Repeat action of beats 5–8 above; on beats 7–8 raise right hands over follow's head while she turns one-half left to face lead
1–4	Lead rocks forward left, backward right, cha, cha, cha; follow rocks forward left, backward right and on beats 3–4 cha, cha, cha turning one-half right under right hands to Varsouvienne position
5–8	Lead rocks backward right, forward left, cha, cha, cha; follow rocks backward right, forward left, and on beats 7–8 cha, cha, cha turning one-half left to face lead
1–4	Lead rocks forward left, backward right, cha cha, cha; follow rocks backward left, forward right, cha, cha, cha turning one-half right on beats 3–4 to Varsouvienne position
5–8	Both rock backward right, forward left, cha, cha, cha

Country Waltz

METER: 3/4. Directions are presented in beats.

BEATS: Country Waltz, a steady 3/4 beat.
Slow: "Alibis," Tracy Laurence CD: *The Best of Tracy Laurence Song.* 100 BPM
Medium: "Drift Off To Dream," Travis Tritt CD: *Country Club Song.* 120 BPM
Fast: "five dollar fine," Chris Le Doux CD: *Stampede Song.* 130 BPM

(Closed position, lead facing line of direction.)

Directions are for the lead, the follow's part is reversed.

BEATS	STEPS	RHYTHM CUE
1	Traveling forward, beginning L, step forward	long
2	Step R forward	short
3	Step L forward	short
4	Step R forward	short
5	Step L forward	short
6	Step R forward	short

NOTE: Body position is important. Shoulders are always parallel. Lead's right arm is firm, wrapped around the follow's back. The lead steers (leads) with his left or right arm, pushing forward.

■ *Variations*

OPEN POSITION

(Closed position)

BEATS	STEPS
1–4	Traveling forward step left, right, left, right
5–6	Change to open position, facing line of direction; step left, right
1–4	Traveling forward, step left, right, left, right
5–6	Resume closed position; lead steps forward left, right; leading the follow to face the lead with the follow's back to the line of direction.

RIGHT PARALLEL POSITION

(Closed position)

BEATS	STEPS
1–2	Lead moves into right parallel, stepping left, right
3–6	Both travel forward clockwise, stepping on each beat
1–2	Turning towards each other to left parallel position, left hips side by side
3–5	Travel forward counterclockwise
6	Lead moves to closed position, facing line of direction stepping right

TURNING WALTZ CLOCKWISE

(Closed position)
Refer to page 22, Waltz Turn.

TRADITIONAL TWO-STEP

Refer to pages 86–87 for various dance positions (Varsouvienne, Little Window, Yoke). These variations may be danced in the Waltz, using 3/4 time.

5

LINE DANCE

L INE DANCE AS A specific dance form has become widely popular. It flourishes with equal enthusiasm in schools, dance halls, clubs, and senior centers. Its chief attraction lies in the fact that since a partner is not required, everyone can participate. Formations are equally unencumbered, ranging from dancers simply scattered about the floor all facing one direction to lines and circles.

Line dancing, or nonpartner dance, has enjoyed an extensive and rich history. In addition to its longevity as a dance form, line dancing also facilitates beginning dance instruction. Its value is particularly apparent when starting a unit with line dances and *then* moving to partner dances. The major benefits of line dancing are:

- Everyone is dancing.
- Dancers have a chance to learn and practice uninhibited by a partner.
- Many basic movements may be introduced to the students as a line dance.

Many of the popular novelty and fad dances of the past such as Bunny Hop, Big Apple, and Hokey Pokey are nonpartner line dances. If all the nonpartner dances from various world cultures were added to this mix, we would have to say, without a doubt, that the line dance is the grand dame of dance!

TEACHING TIPS FOR LINE DANCING

1. When applicable, having students move to the colored lines on the gym floor helps organize the class.

2. Students need to be an "arm's distance" apart. This allows them enough space to move and discourages roughhousing.

3. When facing the class, the instructor's movement should be a mirror image to the students' movement. When the students move to their right, the instructor should move to the left.

4. Rotate lines often. The front row moves to the back, and all other lines move forward. Rotating lines provides several benefits:

   - All students will have a chance to be in the front row with a clear view of the instructor and the demonstration of steps.
   - The instructor has an equally good view of all student reactions and progress.
   - Rotation prevents troublemakers from lingering in the back row and creating a disruption.

5. In a large class, the instructor can watch one line at a time and assist as needed. For this technique, after a line has been reviewed by the instructor, the students sit down while maintaining their lines.

6. Many line dances face a different direction or wall on each repetition and are known as *four-wall line dances*. When the dance is repeated facing a new direction, the instructor should move to maintain a position in front of the students. This effort tends to reduce student disorientation. Once the class knows the dance, cueing the steps should be sufficient.

Line dances can be flexible enough to fit a variety of musical tastes and trends catered to class interest. In the mid–1990s line dancing was generally a country western phenomenon, though not all line dancing has a country western character. Dances such as Macarena gained popularity well beyond country western dancers.

LINE DANCE STYLE

The dance reflects the style of music played: Country Western, Disco, Rap, or Pop. In Country Western Line dancing, when the hands are free, the thumbs are hooked near the belt buckle or both hands are overlapped behind the back with palms facing out.

All Shook Up

ALL SHOOK UP was presented at Brainerd, Minnesota in June of 1999 by Gary E. Sanders, University of Missouri–Kansas City, Missouri.

METER: 4/4. Directions presented in beats.

MUSIC: Slow: "2 of a Kind" by Garth Brooks, "You Ain't Much Fun" by Toby Keith, "All I Want Is A Life" by Tim McGraw.

Full Speed: "All Shook Up," *Honeymoon in Vegas* soundtrack. The dance starts exactly 16 beats into the song.

FORMATION: Lines of dancers all facing front, four wall style.

There are two patterns: Wall 1 Patterns 1 & 2
Wall 2 Patterns 1 & 2
Wall 3 Patterns 1 & 2
Wall 4 Pattern 2
Wall 5 Patterns 1 & 2
Wall 6 Pattern 2
Wall 7 Patterns 1 & 2
Ending

BEATS	STEPS
	Pattern 1
1–2	Cross right over left, stepping down on the toe, then heel
3–4	Step out on left, stepping down on the toe, then heel
5–6	Cross right over left, stepping down on the toe, then heel
7–14	Traveling slightly to the right, kick right foot, ball change, four times

Pattern 2

1–2	Point right toe to the side, cross over left
3–4	Point left toe to the side, cross over right
5–6	Point right toe to the side, cross over left
7–8	Point left toe to the side, cross over right

Snap Kicks

9–10	Kick right foot out in front and to the side
11–12	Cha Cha Cha right, left, right
13–14	Kick left foot out in front and to the side
15–16	Cha Cha Cha right, left, right

Swivel

17–18	Swivel to the right: heels, toes, heels, toes
19–20	Put right toe out in front, pivot one half turn to left
21–22	Put right toe out in front, pivot one half turn to left
23–24	Right one quarter turn, stomp right and hold (one count)
25–26	In place stomp left (feet together) and hold (one count)
27–30	Bump hips right, left, right, left "Any Way You Want"

Ending

1–2	Roll hips twice

California Hustle

THE HUSTLE IS WRITTEN in 4/4 time. The accent is on the first beat of each measure. Traditionally the Hustle is danced to 6 counts of music (one and half measures). The tap (touch) step is characteristic of all Hustles.

4/4	/				/	
	tap	step	tap	step	step	step
	Q	Q	S	Q Q S	S	S
	1	2	3	4	5	6

There are many Hustles, some for no partners, others for couples. The *California Hustle* is also called the *Los Angeles Hustle* and, in New York, *Bus Stop*.

METER: 4/4. Directions presented in beats.

RECORDS: High/Scope RM9; DC 74528.

CASSETTE: High/Scope RM9.

MUSIC: Betty White Records, How to Hustle D115.

FORMATION: Free formation, all facing music. No partners.

(Starting position: feet together, weight on left.)

BEATS	STEPS
	Back and Forward Steps
1–3	Beginning right, take three steps backward
4	Tap left foot to right foot or point left toe backward; weight remains on right
5–7	Beginning left, take three steps forward
8	Tap right foot to the left foot or point left toe forward; weight remains on left
9–12	Repeat steps 1–4
	Grapevine to Side
1	Step left to left side
2	Step right, crossing in front of left
3	Step left to left side
4	Tap right toe to left foot; weight remains on left
5	Step right to right side
6	Step left, crossing in front of right
7	Step right to right side
8	Tap left toe to right foot; weight remains on right
9–10	Step left to left side; tap right to left—no weight
11–12	Step right to right side; tap left to right—no weight

Take a quarter-turn to left to face a new direction and repeat dance

Cowboy Boogie

COWBOY BOOGIE, also called *Country Boogie,* is a Country Western Line Dance.

METER: 4/4, medium to fast. Directions are presented in beats.

MUSIC: "Friends in Low Places," or popular 4/4 country western tune.

FORMATION: Scattered, all facing music.

BEATS	STEPS
1–4	Grapevine. Beginning right, step sideward, cross left behind right, step sideward right, scuff left heel forward and clap
5–8	Repeat grapevine beginning left
9–10	Step right in place, scuff left heel
11–12	Step left in place, scuff right heel
13–16	Moving backwards, step right, left, right, and lift left knee up (hitch)
17–18	Rock forward left, touch right in back
19–20	Rock backward right, touch left in front
21–24	Rock forward left, rock back right, rock forward left, pivoting on left foot, one-quarter turn left and swing right knee up (hitch)

Electric Slide

Electric slide was first danced in 1990 to a pop song, "Electric Boogie." Soon after, the Electric Slide also gained popularity in Country Western Line Dance circles.

METER: 4/4, medium to fast. Directions are presented in beats.

MUSIC: "Electric Boogie" or any popular song.

FORMATION: Lines of dancers, all facing front.

BEATS	STEPS
1–4	Beginning right, step sideward right, close left to right, step sideward right, close left to right, step touch
5–8	Repeat same action to left
9–12	Moving backward, step right, close left to right, step right and touch left heel to right foot
13–14	Rock forward left, touch right (dig) in place; may swing right arm in arc, bending over, and touch floor in front of left foot on the "dig"
15–16	Rock backward right, touch left (dig) in place
17–18	Step left (count one), pivoting on left one-quarter turn left and brush right foot forward (count two)

▪ Variations

1–4	Take three fast slides to right, letting left foot drag, step right, touch left. Repeat to left.
1–4	Or grapevine right (right, left, right), touch left heel. Repeat left.

STYLE: Bend knees on grapevine.

ELECTRIC SLIDE TO FUNK MUSIC

MUSIC: Any popular Funk tune.

STYLE: Bring knees up high. Bend elbows and work arms like a hammer alternately. On the rock, twist shoulders and torso forward and back. Add hops, at every opportunity. Whole body makes exaggerated moves to the music.

Freeze

Freeze is a Country Western Line Dance.

METER: 4/4, medium fast. Directions presented in beats.

RECORD: MH 37.

CASSETTE: MH C37.

MUSIC: Suggested tunes: "Tulsa Line," "Swingin'," "Elvira."

FORMATION: Line of dancers, all facing forward.

BEATS	STEPS
1–4	Grapevine: beginning left, step left sideward; step right behind left; step sidewards left; lift right knee turned out, crossing right heel in front of left, then kick right foot out
5–8	Grapevine: beginning right, repeat action of measures 1–4 to the right
9–12	Traveling backward, step back left, right, left; lift right knee turned out, crossing right heel in front of left, then kick right foot out
13–14	Rock; step forward right, touch left to right; step backward left, touch right to left
15–16	Turning one-quarter turn right, pivot on right foot with left knee bent, foot off the floor, touch left to right; weight remains on right; left foot is free

■ Variations

1. Funky or Hip Hop music. Use upper body and arms, turning shoulders left and right. Lift knees high.
2. Zydeco Music. Upper torso quiet, footwork subtle. Merengue step and body action.

Para Bailar*

Para Bailar (In Order to Dance) presents an easy line dance as choreographed by Henry "Buzz" Glass, January 1997. It uses Caribbean rhythms with a dose of Latin patterns to form a delightful dance recalling a deep blue sea and sculptured palm trees with a splash of greenness.

RECORD: Limbo Rock, Challenge #45–9131

FORMATION: Lines of dancers all facing front, may be done "four wall style" or facing front and back wall alternately.

METER: 2/4

---

* Para Bailar included by permission of Henry "Buzz" Glass, Oakland, California.

Part I: Beguine Basic/Samba Balance

1–2   Beguine Basic: stand with feet about a foot apart. Bending slightly forward, step left in place (count 1), leaning sideward left, touch right ball of foot sideward about a foot apart (count and) step left in place (count 2). Now step right directly under body (count 1), lean sideward right and touch left ball of foot left sideward (count and), then step right in place (count 2). There is an easy sway and accent of hip movement.

3–4   Samba Balance: balance forward with a Two-Step (flat-toe-flat), left, right, left (counts 1 and 2) and then backward, right, left, right (counts 1 and 2).

5–8   Repeat action of measures 1–4.

Part II: Cross Step

1–4   With body bent forward, move sideward right with 7 steps crossing left (flat foot) over the ball of right foot with short rapid steps (left, right, left, right, left, right, left) (2 measures). Reverse direction, move sideward left with right (flat) in front of left (2 measures). Movement has the feeling of a buzz step with slight movement in hips and knees.

Part III: Twisty Two-Step

5–8   Accenting movement with the sway of arms at waist level, move forward with twisty Two-Step (left, right, left) (flat-toe-flat) (counts 1 and 2), then right, left, right (counts 1 and 2). Making a quarter turn left, use the same pattern left, right, left and right, left, right (2 measures) to face a new wall (Four Corners).

Saturday Night Fever Line Dance

THIS DANCE CONTAINS many of the disco dance steps that were made popular by the movie *Saturday Night Fever.*

METER: 4/4

MUSIC: "Staying Alive"

FORMATION: Lines of dancers, all facing front.

BEATS	STEPS
	Walks forward and back
1–4	Walk back; beginning right, step back right, left, right, touch left foot to right and clap
5–8	Repeat walking forward, beginning left
9–16	Repeat actions of counts 1–8
	Walks side, turns side
1–4	Walk side; beginning right, walk to the right, right, left, right, touch left foot to right and clap
5–8	Repeat walking left, beginning left
9–12	Three step turn to the right; beginning right, turn 90° to right, step forward right, pivoting 90° clockwise, on right foot, step side left on left (end facing back wall); pivoting 180° clockwise on left foot, step side right on right; end facing front; touch left foot to right and clap
13–16	Three step turn to the left; repeat action of counts 9–12 to the left
	Roll It *(feet are shoulder width apart)*
1–2	With hands at waist level, roll them around in a counterclockwise motion
3–4	Reach behind the back and clap twice
5–8	Repeat actions of counts 1–4

STYLE: Move hips to the right on counts 1–2 and left on counts 3–4

	Point
1	Lift right arm, side high right, pointing up with index finger
2	Cross the right arm in front of the body, pointing side left low
3–6	Repeat actions of count 1 and 2 twice
	Funky Chicken
	Arms are raised, with hands in a fist by shoulders, elbows are dropped to the side, in a wing flapping motion on counts 7 and 8
7	Rise up on ball of the feet, toes together and heels out; click heel together
8	Repeat action of count 7
	Heel Toe
1	Touch right heel in front
2	Repeat
3	Touch right toe behind
4	Repeat
5	Touch right heel in front
6	Touch right toe behind
7	Step forward on right (leaving left in place)
8	Pivoting on right foot 90° counterclockwise, slide left foot to right

Slappin' Leather

§LAPPIN' LEATHER IS A Country Western Line Dance choreographed by Gayle Brandon.

METER: 4/4, medium to fast. Directions presented in beats.

MUSIC: Suggested tunes: "Elvira," "Tulsa Times," "Swingin'," "Baby's Got Her Blue Jeans On."

FORMATION: Line of dancers, all face front.

BEATS	STEPS
1–4	Swivel, weight on balls of feet; spread heels apart, heels together; spread heels apart, heels together
5–8	Touch right heel forward, step right in place; touch left heel forward, step left in place
9–12	Repeat action of beats 5–8
13–14	Tap right heel in front twice, foot turned out
15–16	Tap right toe in back twice
17–20	Star: Touch right toe forward, to right side, behind left, and to right side
21	Slap leather: Weight remains on left; swing right foot behind left and slap right boot with left hand
22	While turning a quarter turn left (pivot on left foot), swing right foot to right side and slap right boot with right hand
23	Swing right foot in front of left and slap right boot with left hand
24	Swing right foot to right side and slap right boot with right hand
25–28	Grapevine: Beginning right, step right, step left behind right, step sideward right, chug (scoot) right, lifting left knee up (hitch), and clap hands
29–32	Beginning left, repeat action of beats 23–26 to the left
33–36	Traveling backward, step right, left, right, chug (scoot) right, lifting left foot behind right leg and slap left heel with right hand
37–38	Step forward left, close right next to left; weight on both feet
39–40	Step forward left, stomp on right foot next to left, weight on both feet

STYLE: Review Line Dance style for California Hustle, page 93.

Twelfth Street Rag

TWELFTH STREET RAG is a novelty dance composed to a popular tune.

METER: 4/4

RECORDS: DC 74505; High/Scope RM5.

CASSETTES: DC 15X; High/Scope RM5.

FORMATION: Single circle, hands joined; scattered; or lines of four to five, hands joined, facing line of direction.

STEPS: Strut, Charleston, grapevine.

MEASURES	STEPS
1	Beginning left, strut four steps forward
2	Point left toe forward, then to side; beginning left, take three steps backward
3–4	Beginning right, repeat action of measures 1–2
5	Beginning left, take seven quick steps sideward to left; type of step options could be shuffle, step close, grapevine, and swivel steps
6	Beginning right, take seven quick steps sideward to right
7–8	Beginning left, take two Charleston steps in place
	Repeat dance
	Interlude
1	Jump forward on both feet, throwing hands up in air; jump backwards on both feet, throwing hands back, turn and face the other way
2	Turn individually to own right, taking three steps (strut right, left, right) and clap own hands on fourth count; improvise during interlude

6

LATIN DANCES

Cha Cha

A CUBAN INNOVATION of the old basic Latin form (danson), the *Cha Cha* is said to be a combination of the Mambo and American Swing. A close look shows its rhythm to be that of a Triple Mambo, its style that of the Rumba, and its open swingy variations that of the Triple Time Swing. It does not have as heavy a quality or as large a foot pattern as the Mambo; nor has it the smooth sophistication or the conservative figures of the Rumba. It reflects a light, breezy mood, a carefree gaiety, and a trend in the challenge steps for dancers to ad–lib variations to their heart's content. Consequently one sees variations in almost every known position.

CHA CHA RHYTHM

In 4/4 time, the catchy rhythm and delightful music of the Cha Cha have brought dancers and musicians alike a new treat in the undeniably Latin flavor. The rhythm has been a controversy. Originally it was done on the offbeat of the measure, and then there was a widespread acceptance of the onbeat rhythm, which is the easier way, but again the trend is to go back to the offbeat rhythm. Analysis in this edition will be done with the offbeat rhythm.

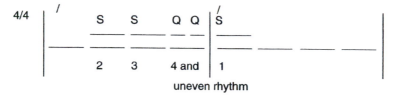

The rhythm is an uneven beat pattern of slow slow quick quick slow and will be counted 2 3 4 *and* 1, with the 4 *and* 1 being the familiar Cha Cha Cha triple. Rhythmically the beats are as follows:

cha cha cha

Note that the last beat of the triple is a quarter note, not an eighth note as is sometimes misinterpreted.

CHA CHA STYLE

The Cha Cha is seen danced in a variety of positions as it moves in and out of the variations. However, the three basic positions are closed position, face–to–face position, and challenge position (which is completely apart from but facing partner). Beginners like the facing position with two hands joined. The follow holds her arms up with the elbows just in front of her body. The hands are up, fingers pointing inward. The lead reaches over the top of the follow's forefingers and grasps her fingers with his fingers and thumb. The follow exerts a little resistance against his fingers. Both lead and follow hold the forearms firm so that the lead can push, pull, or turn her, and she responds, not with arm motion or shoulder rotation, but with body motion forward, back, or turning. The arm and hand, when free, are held up parallel to the floor in bent–arm position, and they turn with the body as it moves.

The Cha Cha, with its light bouncy quality, is delightfully Latin as it carries with it some of the subtleness of the Rumba movement. The forward foot should be placed nearly flat on the floor. The knee is bent over the stepping foot. The back step (instead of a flat step that tends to give the appearance of a sag) is a toe step, holding the body firmly so as to avoid the sag. The Cha Cha triple is taken with very small steps in place or traveling but is kept close to the floor. The upper body is held comfortably upright and the head focuses on one's partner in a typical gracious Latin manner. The eye contact brings the dance to life.

FUNDAMENTAL CHA CHA STEPS

Directions are for the lead, facing line of direction; the follow's part is reverse, except as noted.

BACK BASIC STEP

(Challenge or Two hands joined)

STEPS	4/4 COUNTS	RHYTHM CUE
Step L sideways (preliminary step)	1	slow
Step R backward	2	slow
Step L forward in place	3	slow
Step R in place next to L	4	quick (cha)
Step L in place	and	quick (cha)
Step R in place	1	slow (cha)

NOTE: There is a side step on the accented first beat to begin the dance only, and it is not used again.

FORWARD BASIC STEP

STEPS	4/4 COUNTS	RHYTHM CUE
Step L forward	2	slow
Step R back in place	3	slow
Step L in place next to R	4	quick (cha)
Step R in place	and	quick (cha)
Step L in place	1	slow (cha)

STEP CUE: Back forward Cha Cha Cha/forward back Cha Cha Cha.

STYLE: The back basic has the toe step, the forward basic has the flat style (see Cha Cha Cha style). Dancers have a tendency to pound the feet on the floor for the Cha Cha Cha. It should be neither a pounding nor scuffing sound.

LEAD: The lead leads by pulling with his right hand going into the back basic or pushing with the left hand going into the forward basic. If arm and elbow are firm, finger resistance aids in getting the message across. The body should respond by moving backward or forward.

POSITION: The basic Cha Cha may be done in closed, facing, or challenge position.

NOTE: This is the basic step of Cha Cha. The forward half is also called the "forward break"; the back half is the "back break." They may be used with either foot leading when called for in a particular variation. Sometimes the Cha Cha part of the step is used to travel rather than being in place.

■ *Cha Cha Step Variations*

Open Break	Return to Basic	Full Turn	Shadow
Right Break	Cross Over Turn	Jody Break	Kick Swivel
Cross Over	Chase Half-Turn	Reverse Jody	Kick Freeze

OPEN BREAK

(Two hands joined or Latin social position)

The purpose of the break is to change position from face to face to side by side. The couple may open to either right or left. The right break is described next.

RIGHT BREAK

STEPS	4/4 COUNTS	RHYTHM CUE
Step R backward, releasing R hand hold with follow	2	slow
Step L forward in place	3	slow
Step R in place, turning one-quarter clockwise to face R in a side-by-side position	4	quick
Step L in place	*and*	quick
Step R in place	1	slow

STEP CUE: Break open turn Cha Cha Cha.

STYLE: The released hand and arm remain up in place and turn with the body.

LEAD: The lead releases right hand or right turn, left hand for left turn, and guides through to the side–by–side position with the other joined hand. As the lead does this, the follow should exert slight resistance against his arm with her arm or wrist to facilitate following forthcoming leads in side–by–side position.

NOTE: The left break will start forward with the left foot and turn one–quarter left.

CROSS OVER

(Side–by–side position, having taken the open break to the right)

Lead's left is holding follow's right hand. Start with the inside foot (lead's left, follow's right).

STEPS	4/4 COUNTS	RHYTHM CUE
Step L forward	2	slow
Step R back in place	3	slow
Step L in place, turning to face follow, and release her R hand	4	quick
Step R in place, still turning on around, take follow's L hand	*and*	quick
Step L in place, finishing a half-turn to face opposite direction in side-by-side position	1	slow
Repeat, starting with the inside foot (lead's right, follow's left) and turning back to starting position.		

STEP CUE: Forward turn Cha Cha Cha.

STYLE: On the forward step, the inside foot should step straight ahead. The body is upright and the head is looking over the inside shoulder at partner. The free hand is up. Avoid bouncing, leaning forward, turning back on partner, or looking at the floor.

LEAD: The lead's inside hand guides forward into the forward step and pulls back to start the turn. If the arms of both lead and follow remain up when turning, the arms are ready to receive the lead when changing from one hand to the other.

NOTE: If the open break was taken to the left side, then the cross over step will begin with the inside foot (lead's right, follow's left). The cross over step may be repeated from side to side any number of times.

RETURN TO BASIC

(Side–by–side position, facing right starting with the inside foot)

STEPS	4/4 COUNTS	RHYTHM CUE
Step L forward	2	slow
Step R backward in place, turning to face partner	3	slow
Step L, R, L in place taking both of the follow's hands	4 *and* 1	quick quick slow
With R foot now free, go into a back basic		

LEAD: If the lead uses pressure against the follow's fingers of the hand he holds just before he takes both hands, she will recognize the intent to go back to basic and will facilitate the transition.

CROSS OVER TURN

(Side by side, facing left, starting with the inside foot [lead's right, follow's left])

STEPS	4/4 COUNTS	RHYTHM CUE
Step R forward, turning counterclockwise away from the follow about halfway around	2	slow
Step L in place, continuing to turn counterclockwise, completing the turn around to face the follow	3	slow
Bring feet together and hold	4 *and* 1	quick quick slow
Free the L foot and step into a forward basic on count 2		

STEP CUE: Out around *hold* Cha Cha Cha/forward step Cha Cha Cha.

STYLE: A smooth spin on the ball of the foot is taken on counts 2 and 3 and then a sudden hold during the Cha Cha Cha part gives this variation a bit of special pizazz. It is necessary to count the timing carefully so as to step forward into basic again on count 2. The follow is turning clockwise.

LEAD: The lead, knowing he is going into the cross over turn, will not grasp the follow's hand as he comes through from the other side but will place the heel of his hand against the back of her hand and push out slightly into the turn. He must then direct her into a back basic as he steps into his forward basic.

NOTE: Of course, the turn may be taken from either side. The lead may use this variation as a lead into challenge position, in which case he will not rejoin hands with partner but will remain apart, facing partner.

CHASE HALF-TURN

(Challenge position or Two hands joined)

It is a turning figure in which the lead is always one turn ahead of the follow. He will start the turn while she takes a back basic. On her next forward basic she starts the turn. After the desired number of turns he will finish with a forward basic while she completes her last turn to face him. The forward break is used with alternating feet for all turns.

STEPS	4/4 COUNTS	RHYTHM CUE
Lead's Part		
Step L forward, turning clockwise on both feet halfway around with back to follow	2	slow
Take weight on R foot	3	slow
Step L, R, L in place	4 *and* 1	quick quick slow
Step R forward, turning counterclockwise a half turn, on both feet, to face follow's back	2	slow
Take weight on L foot	3	slow
Step R, L, R in place	4 *and* 1	quick quick slow
Follow's Part		
Step R backward	2	slow
Step L forward in place	3	slow
Step R, L, R in place	4 *and* 1	quick quick slow
Step L forward, turning clockwise on both feet halfway around with back to lead	2	slow
Take weight on R foot	3	slow
Step L, R, L in place	4 *and* 1	quick quick slow

STEP CUE: Turn about Cha Cha Cha.

STYLE: The turn about is called a swivel turn and is done with both feet in an apart position. The step is forward, the swivel turns toward the back foot, with the weight on the balls of the feet. There is a cocky manner as lead and follow look over the shoulder at partner.

LEAD: The lead drops both hands when stepping forward left foot, and the rest is a visual lead for the follow. She keeps turning if he does. When the lead wishes to go back to basic, he will take a forward basic while she does her last turn and then rejoin hands and go into a back basic on the right foot.

NOTE: The half turn may be done again and again. A familiar styling is to tap partner's shoulder when facing partner's back.

FULL TURN

(Challenge position)

Step left forward, pivoting clockwise a half turn. Step right in place, again pivoting clockwise a half turn. Take Cha Cha Cha in place, facing partner.

LEAD: The lead is a visual one, having let go of hands to start the turn and taking the hands to finish it.

STYLE: The manner is a bit cocky as each looks over the shoulder at partner. The pivoting steps are small and on the ball of the foot for good balance and smoothness.

NOTE: The lead will make a complete turn while the follow does a back basic, and then she follows with a complete turn while he does a back basic.

JODY BREAK

(Two hands joined)

STEPS	4/4 COUNTS	RHYTHM CUE
Lead's Part:		
Step L backward, and at the same time changing hands from a two-hand grasp to a right-hand grasp	2	slow
Step R forward, and at the same time pull with the R hand to guide the follow into a counterclockwise turn	3	slow
Take Cha Cha Cha (L, R, L) in place, guiding the follow into Varsouvienne position	4 *and* 1	quick quick slow
Step R backward in Varsouvienne position	2	slow
Step L forward in place and, at the same time, release the left hand and guide the follow with the R hand to turn clockwise	3	slow
Take Cha Cha Cha (R, L, R) in place, guiding the follow back out to original position, facing lead completing half turn clockwise	4 *and* 1	quick quick slow

NOTE: This may be repeated over and over without changing the right-hand grasp. When the lead desires to go back to regular basic, he will change to two-hand grasp and forward basic when the follow returns to facing position.

Follow's Part: Starting right foot into regular back break.

Step R backward, allowing lead to change from two-hand grasp to a R-hand grasp	2	slow
Step L forward, toeing out and pivoting on L counterclockwise, being guided by lead's lead toward Varsouvienne position	3	slow
Take Cha Cha Cha (R, L, R), finishing the turn into Varsouvienne position beside the lead	4 *and* 1	quick quick slow
Step L backward in Varsouvienne position	2	slow
Step R forward, toeing out and pivoting on the R clockwise, being guided by the lead's lead towards the original facing position	3	slow
Take Cha Cha Cha (L, R, L) in place finishing the turn to face partner	4 *and* 1	quick quick slow

STEP CUE: Back forward Cha Cha Cha.

STYLE: Both lead and follow should keep steps small and not get too far apart. Large steps and big movement spoil the beauty of this lovely figure and make it awkward to maneuver.

LEAD: Arm tension control makes it possible for the lead's lead to guide the follow smoothly in and out of Varsouvienne position.

VARIATIONS FROM JODY POSITION

(Also called Varsouvienne position)

1. **Reverse Jody:** While in Varsouvienne position, both break back on the inside foot, and while stepping forward turn one-half clockwise in place to reverse Varsouvienne, with the follow on the left of the lead, and take Cha Cha Cha in place. Repeat, starting with the inside foot, and turn counterclockwise to end up in original position. This may be repeated any number of times. Steps are very small. Both partners are using back break continuously.

2. **Shadow:** While in Varsouvienne position, both break on the inside foot, then releasing the Varsouvienne grasp, step forward, the lead guiding the follow across in front of him. Take the Cha Cha Cha, finishing the cross over, and catch inside hands. Follow is to left of lead. Repeat, starting with the inside foot and crossing the follow in front of the lead to a hand-grasp position on his right. This may be repeated any number of times. Return to Varsouvienne position with the follow on the right when ready to go back to a facing position and back to a regular basic.

STYLE: In the Shadow, couples do not get farther apart than a bent-elbow control. The footwork in the apart position changes on count 2 to a back-cross style; that is, the inside foot crosses behind the standing foot. The action of the changing sides with partner is done on the Cha Cha Cha beats like a running motion.

STEP CUE: Cross step Cha Cha Cha.

LEAD: The lead leads with his fingers, pulling her on count 4.

NOTE: The lead may lead the follow across in front of him or in back of him.

KICK SWIVEL

(Two hands joined)

STEPS	4/4 COUNTS	RHYTHM CUE
Step L sideward	2	slow
Kick R across in front of L	3	slow
Put both feet together and swivel both toes to the R and then both heels to the R	4 *and* 1	slow slow
Repeat stepping R sideward	2	slow
Kick L across in front of R	3	slow
Put both feet together and swivel both toes to the L and then both heels to the L	4 *and* 1	slow slow
Return to basic from either side by using the free foot, if left to lead a forward basic, if right to lead a back basic.		

STEP CUE: Step kick swivel swivel.

STYLE: Dancers should take small steps. Keep the kick low and take the swivel steps with the feet and knees close together. One may bend the knees slightly. The lead and follow kick in the same direction.

LEAD: The lead pulls both of the follow's hands in the direction of the step kick, and then he puts the hands close together and gives a push–pull action for the swivel. Part of the lead the follow picks up visually.

NOTE: The two swivel steps take the place of the three cha cha cha steps and are even rhythm, being the equivalent of counts 4 and 1.

KICK FREEZE

(Facing position or Latin social position)

STEPS	4/4 COUNTS	RHYTHM CUE
Step L sideward	2	slow
Kick R across in front of L	3	slow
Touch R foot sideward to the R in a stride position (no weight change); count 4—hold count 1	4, 1	slow slow
Step R, L, R, moving to the R without changing position	2 *and* 3	quick quick slow
Repeat on the same foot	4, 1, 2, 3, 4, *and* 1	

STEP CUE: The posture on the freeze straightens to be extra firm and holds with the leg extended sideward. Arms extend sideward to butterfly position. The body may turn slightly to the right during the Cha Cha Cha but should end up facing partner.

LEAD: The lead pulls both of the follow's hands in the direction of the kick and then suddenly increases tension as arms and legs swing to freeze position. They hold the position 1 beat. Then he releases pressure and leads sideward for the quick slow beats.

NOTE: The freeze is on counts 4 and 1. These are two extra counts added to the regular pattern. It is best to take the kick freeze twice to make it fit rhythmically with the music. Return to basic by leading into a back basic with the right foot.

CHA CHA COMBOS

The Cha Cha routines are combinations for practice, listed from simple to complex. (Partners facing, unless otherwise indicated.)

1. *Open Break and Cross Over*
   2 forward and back basics
      with open break
   4 cross overs
2. *Cross Over With Turn*
   2 basics with open break
   3 cross overs and turn
      repeat
3. *Cross Over and Freeze*
   2 basics with open break
   2 cross overs
   2 freeze
   1 cross over and turn

4. *Basic and Chase*
   2 basics
   4 half turns
   2 full turns
5. *Basic and Jody*
   2 basics
   4 jody breaks

6. *Jody Variations*
   2 basics
   jody break
   2 double jody
   2 shadow
7. *Basic and Kick Freeze*
   2 basics (closed position)
   2 kick freeze

Mambo

THE *MAMBO* IS A Cuban dance that appeared on the ballroom scene in the United States shortly after World War II. It is a very free dance allowing for individual interpretation and innovation. Probably due to its difficult rhythm, it became less popular in the 1950s than the Cha Cha Cha. However, it did survive and finds renewed interest among dancers in the United States, especially the advanced dancer. Over the years it has become more sophisticated and conservative. It is most often done in closed position.

MAMBO RHYTHM

The rhythm is difficult and has spurred controversy as to whether the rhythm is off–beat or onbeat, that is, quick quick slow or slow quick quick. Because of its highly syncopated beat, it has been a difficult rhythm to learn. The rhythm pattern described here will be in 4/4 time, that is, quick quick slow.

4/4 | —— —— —— ——
    | 4   1   2   Hold

A preparation step on the first two beats of the measure is helpful in getting started with the Mambo beat.

4/4 | —— —— ——   —— —— —— ——
    | 1   2   Hold   4   1   2   Hold
    | Preparation   Mambo Rhythm

MAMBO STYLE

The sultry rhythm and oddly accented beat gives the dance a heavy jerky quality, which may be interestingly thought of as a "charge." Basically, the style is Rumba movement, but as one steps forward on the accented fourth beat, it is with the suddenness of a quick lunge but immediately pulling back for the second quick beat, giving the jerky quality to the dance. The "charge" movement is further accented by a slightly heavier step and the action of the shoulders which move forward alternately in opposition to the stepping foot. The arms and hands are carried in a bent elbow position parallel to the floor, palms down. The arms move the shoulders, and thus the Mambo presents a more dynamic body movement than any of the other Cuban dances.

FUNDAMENTAL MAMBO STEPS

Only the basic step will be given here since all variations may be taken from the Cha Cha. The relationship between the Mambo and the Cha Cha will also be noted. Cha Cha variations may be found on pages 103–108. Directions are for the lead, facing the line of direction; follow's part is reverse, except as noted.

Preparation Step (Used only at the beginning of the dance to get started on the Mambo beat)

STEPS	4/4 COUNTS	RHYTHM CUE
Step L in place	1	quick
Step R in place	2	quick
Hold	3	hold

THE BASIC STEP		
Step L diagonally forward to R	4	quick
Step R back in place	1	quick
Step L sideward L	2	slow
Hold, closing R to L	3	no weight change
Step R diagonally backward to L	4	quick
Step L back in place	1	quick
Step R sideward R	2	slow
Hold closing L to R	3	no weight change

STEP CUE: Cross back side, cross back side.

STYLE: Dancers should avoid taking too large a step. The sideward step tends to increase the size of the total pattern and may look very awkward if taken too wide. The quality is sultry.

LEAD: The lead's lead is a sharp shoulder action as his shoulder moves forward in opposition to the stepping foot. The follow should merely follow the action of his leading shoulder and not try to figure out which shoulder to move.

POSITION: Latin social position

NOTE: The first half of this step is referred to as the "forward break" and the back half as the "back break." It may be used as in the Cha Cha.

■ *Mambo Variations*

These variations are fully described in the Cha Cha found on pages 103–108. Also refer to Cha Cha Combos on page 108–109.

Open Break   Cross Over Turn   Shadow
Cross Over   Jody Break

NOTE: In making the transition from Cha Cha to Mambo one must keep in mind the relationship between the two rhythms.

Merengue

THIS CLEVER LITTLE DANCE from the Caribbean could very well be a favorite with the young adult set if they really had a chance to explore it. The music is a peppy, pert, marchlike rhythm, and the dance patterns are the most simple of all the Latin dances. There are two styles: the original "limp step" from the Dominican Republic and the more even, smooth Haitian style. The Haitian style will be described here.

MERENGUE RHYTHM

In 4/4 time, there is a very pronounced beat of the music, which has an exciting uneven beat in the rhythm pattern, but the dance follows the basic beats of the measure and is in even rhythm.

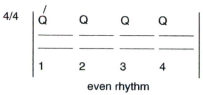

even rhythm

MERENGUE STYLE

Perhaps Merengue style could be described as a combination of the Rumba movement and a majorette swagger step. The feet are placed flat, but the weight is on the ball of the foot for easy balance. It is a controlled hip movement resulting from the bent–knee action with each step as in the Rumba, but it has the almost sassy quality and breezy manner of the majorette. A slight rock sideways with the shoulders to accompany the foot pattern is optional. It is not meant to be an exaggerated body movement, but the lively music and the character of the step give this dance a delightful touch of humor.

With a simple step, the footwork must be disciplined or it may look sloppy. The feet face squarely forward and close tightly together. The step is small.

FUNDAMENTAL MERENGUE STEPS

Directions are for the lead; the follow's part is reversed, except as noted.

BASIC SIDE STEP

(Latin social position)

STEPS	4/4 COUNTS	RHYTHM CUE
Step L sideward	1	quick
Close R to L, take weight on R	2	quick
Step L sideward	3	quick
Close R to L, take weight on R	4	quick

STEP CUE: Side close.

STYLE: Steps are small, head high, focus on partner. Rock body left, right with the step.

LEAD: To lead a sideward moving pattern in closed position, the lead should use pressure of the right hand to the left or right to indicate the desired direction.

NOTE: Could travel sideways any number of side steps. Should travel in line of direction.

BOX STEP

(Latin social position)

STEPS	4/4 COUNTS	RHYTHM CUE
Step L forward	1	quick
Close R to L, take weight on R	2	quick
Step L backward	3	quick
Close R to L, take weight on R	4	quick

STEP CUE: Forward together back together.

STYLE: The same foot leads each time. The shoulders lead the rock from side to side.

LEAD: To lead a box step the lead should use a forward body action followed by right–hand pressure and right elbow pull to the right to take the follow into the forward sequence of the box. Forward pressure of the right hand followed by pressure to the left side takes the follow into the back sequence of the box.

BOX TURN

(Latin social position)

STEPS	4/4 COUNTS	RHYTHM CUE
Step L, toeing out to a L one-quarter turn counterclockwise	1	quick
Close R to L, take weight on R	2	quick
Step L backward	3	quick
Close R to L, take weight on R	4	quick

STEP CUE: Turn close back close.

STYLE: A shoulder rock on the turn makes it very easy to lead.

LEAD: See lead indication 6, page 14.

NOTE: Repeat three times to make a full turn.

CROSS STEP

(Latin social position)

STEPS	4/4 COUNTS	RHYTHM CUE
Step L sideward, turning to open position	1	quick
Step R forward, in open position	2	quick
Step L sideward, turning to closed position	3	quick
Close R to L, take weight on R	4	quick

STEP CUE: Open step side close.

STYLE: Each step must be precisely taken in the closed or open position. If the footwork is not square with each position, the merengue loses all of its distinctive character.

LEAD: To lead into an open position or conversation position, the lead should use pressure with the heel of the right hand to turn the follow into open position. The right elbow lowers to the side. The lead must simultaneously turn his own body, not just the follow, so that they end facing the same direction. The left arm relaxes slightly and the left hand sometimes gives the lead for steps in the open position.

LEAD: To lead from open to closed position the lead should use pressure of the right hand and raise the right arm up to standard position to move the follow into closed position. The follow should not have to be pushed but should swing easily into closed position as she feels the arm lifting. She should move completely around to face the lead squarely.

VARIATION: The flick is like the cross step, except that there is a *leap* onto the left foot in open position, bending the right knee and flipping the right foot quickly up in back, and then right foot steps forward and side close as above. The lead raises his right elbow as he turns to open position into the leap.

SWIVEL

(Open and closed traveling in line of direction)

STEPS	4/4 COUNTS	RHYTHM CUE
Leap L forward in open position flick R foot	1	quick
Step R forward in open position	2	quick
Pivot on R foot to face partner, bringing L foot alongside of R, shift weight to L	3	quick
Pivot on L foot to open position, bringing R foot alongside of L, shift weight to R	4	quick
Repeat pivot on R	1	quick
Repeat pivot on L	2	quick
Step L, turning to closed position	3	quick
Close R to L, taking weight R	4	quick

STEP CUE: Leap step, swivel, swivel, swivel, swivel, side close.

STYLE: Steps are tiny and neat, turning exactly a quarter turn each time. The body turns with the foot.

LEAD: To lead into an open position or conversation position, the lead should use pressure with the heel of the right hand to turn the follow into open position. The right elbow lowers to the side. The lead must simultaneously turn his own body, not just the follow, so that they end facing the same direction. The left arm relaxes slightly and the left hand sometimes gives the lead for steps in the open position.

LEAD: To lead from open to closed position the lead should use pressure of the right hand and raise the right arm up to standard position to move the follow into closed position. The follow should not have to be pushed but should swing easily into closed position as she feels the arm lifting. She should move completely around to face the lead squarely.

LADDER

(Latin social position)

STEPS	4/4 COUNTS	RHYTHM CUE
Step L sideward	1	quick
Close R to L, take weight on R	2	quick
Step L forward	3	quick
Close R to L, take weight on R	4	quick

STEP CUE: Side close forward close.

STYLE: Footwork small and neat. Face partner squarely.

LEAD: Moving squarely into position helps lead the body. Since there are a lot of direction changes in the Merengue, the follow must be extremely alert to the action of the lead's right arm and shoulder.

SIDE CLOSE AND BACK BREAK

(Latin social position)

STEPS	4/4 COUNTS	RHYTHM CUE
Step L sideward	1	quick
Close R to L, take weight on R	2	quick
Step L sideward	3	quick
Close R to L, take weight on R	4	quick
Step L sideward	1	quick
Step R, in place, turning to open position	2	quick
Step L backward, in open position	3	quick
Step R, in place, turning to closed position	4	quick

STEP CUE: Side close side close side open back step.

STYLE: There is a rather sudden swing to open position on count 2 of the second measure and then immediately back to closed position on count 4.

LEAD: The lead uses his left hand to push the follow out quickly to open position.

MERENGUE COMBOS

(Closed position)

1. 4 basic steps
   4 box steps
   4 basic steps
   4 box turns

2. 4 basic steps
   4 cross steps
   8 box steps

3. 4 basic steps
   4 box turns
   4 swivels

4. 4 basic steps
   4 ladder
   4 box turns
   4 side close and back break

Rumba

THE LATIN AMERICAN DANCES are to American dancing what garlic is to the good cook. Used sparingly, they can add a tangy interest to our dancing. The *Rumba* is a Cuban dance (along with the Mambo, Bolero, and Cha Cha Cha) but it has enjoyed greater popularity than any of the others, probably because of its slower, more relaxed, smoother style. The music is usually identified by the tantalizing rhythms of the percussion instruments known as the maracas, which carry the continuous quick beat, and the sticks or bongo drum, which beat out the accented rhythm of the dance.

RUMBA RHYTHM

The Rumba is written in 4/4 time and is played both fast and slow. Many Americans prefer the slower Bolero–type tempo, but actually in the Latin American countries the rumba is danced considerably faster. The rhythm is tricky as it is a 1 2 3, 1 2 3, 1 2 count in 4/4 time.

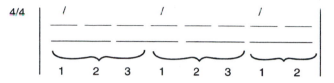

It was taught in the United States for many years as a quick quick slow rhythm, but it has gradually shifted over to a slow quick quick beat with the accent on the first and third beats of the measure. This is the rhythm that will be used in this text.

```
4/4 | S      Q  Q |
    | ---    --- --- |
    | ---    --- --- |
    | 1 – 2  3  4 |
      uneven rhythm
```

Rumba music has a subtle, beautiful melody with a rolling quality that requires the subtle rolling Rumba movement. It is seldom mistaken for the Cha Cha Cha or mambo music because of its smoothness and continuity.

RUMBA STYLE

Naturally, in the transition, the Rumba lost a lot of its original character. The style has been greatly exaggerated and distorted at times. Some people dance it like the Foxtrot, without attempting to get any of the Cuban flavor. It is hoped that dancers will feel sufficiently challenged to put in a little extra time to get the feeling of the subtle, continuous, rolling motion. Three characteristics make it different from other dances:

1. The action is in the feet and the knees.
2. There is a delayed shift of weight.
3. The upper body is upright and quiet, with a focus on one's partner.

The step itself is comparatively short and flat–footed, with the knee leading. The weight tends to be maintained over the heel of the foot more than in any other dance. The Cuban Rumba movement is a springlike action, resulting from placing the left foot on the floor first, without taking weight but with a bent knee. This is followed by pressing the weight into the floor and straightening the left knee. Accompanying this press into the floor, a smooth roll of the weight is shifted to that left foot. The right knee begins to bend and leads the right foot, then free of weight, into its new position. The roll is completed as the weight is transferred gradually to the newly placed right foot. Then the entire action is repeated by pressing the weight into the right foot and straightening the right knee rolling smoothly. As the left foot is freed of weight, the knee leads, shifting the left foot to its new position with the weight coming over it, completing the roll.

The knees should be bent directly over the foot, and the feet should be placed with the toes pointing straight ahead. A pigeon–toed effect should be avoided. As the feet pass each other, the steps are small and close together, with the toes pointed straight ahead in the line of direction. The movement of the hips is merely the subtle result of the specific action of the feet and the knees. There should be no intentional swinging of the hip from side to side. There needs to be a stabilization of the upper trunk at the waist to keep it easily upright and the shoulders straight.

The head is held with the focus constantly on one's partner. The arm and hand, when free from partner, are held in a bent–elbow position, waist level, palm down. The lead does not hold his partner close. There is seldom any body contact.

The Rumba, with its open and encircling patterns, is generally danced within a small space and reflects a dignified, although flirtatious, quality.

■ *Teaching Suggestions for Rumba Style*

First, practice the motion described above, moving forward in a slow slow rhythm, working to achieve the feeling of the roll. Practice in front of a mirror is usually helpful. Second, practice the same motion forward in a slow quick quick rhythm (Cuban walk). Third, practice the motion as in the box step. Finally, practice with partner in closed dance position.

FUNDAMENTAL RUMBA STEPS

Directions are for the lead, facing line of direction; follow's part is reversed, except as noted.

CUBAN WALK

STEPS	4/4 COUNTS	RHYTHM CUE
Place L forward, roll weight slowly onto L	1–2	slow
Place R forward, roll weight quickly onto R	3	quick
Place L forward, roll weight quickly onto L	4	quick

STEP CUE: Place–roll roll roll.
        1 – 2 3 4

STYLE: The roll is the springlike action of pressing into the floor. The knee of the free foot bends and leads the foot into its new position, followed by the transfer of weight to that foot.

NOTE: The Cuban walk step is used for all moving variations when not in closed position. It may move forward, backward, or in a circle.

BOX STEP

(Latin social position)

STEPS	4/4 COUNTS	RHYTHM CUE
Place L forward, roll weight slowly onto L	1–2	slow
Place R sideward, roll weight quickly onto R	3	quick
Place L close to R, roll weight quickly to L	4	quick
Place R backward, roll weight slowly onto R	1–2	slow
Place L sideward, roll weight quickly onto L	3	quick
Place R close to L roll weight quickly onto R	4	quick

STEP CUE: Forward side close/back side close.

STYLE: The knee leads each step. The feet are placed flat on the floor, in a small box pattern.

Floor pattern

start

LEAD: To lead a box step, the lead should use a forward body action followed by right-hand pressure and right elbow pull to the right to take the follow into the forward sequence of the box. Forward pressure of the right hand followed by pressure to the left side takes the follow into the back sequence of the box.

NOTE: Students need to understand that this forward, side, close constitutes the forward sequence or forward basic and that back, side, close constitutes the back sequence or back basic. These will be referred to in the variations.

■ *Rumba Step Variations*

Box Turn	Circular Turn	Walk Around
Flirtation Break	Parallel Turn	Parallel Turn
Side by Side	Bolero Break	

BOX TURN

(Latin social position)

The Rumba box step is the same foot pattern as the Westchester box step in the Fox-trot. The box turn will follow the same pattern as the Foxtrot box turn, page 33. The style is different and one needs to shorten the step and add the Cuban movement.

FLIRTATION BREAK

(Latin social position)

Starting from Latin social position, dancers will change to flirtation position and travel with the Cuban walk either forward or backward.

STEPS	4/4 COUNTS	RHYTHM CUE
Step L forward	1–2	slow
Step R sideward	3	quick
Close L to R, roll weight L	4	quick
Step R backward, a larger step changing to flirtation position, removing his R arm from around partner	1–2	slow
Step L sideward	3	quick
Close R to L, roll weight to R	4	quick
Step L forward	1–2	slow
Step R forward	3	quick
Step L forward	4	quick
Step R forward	1–2	slow
Step L forward	3	quick
Step R forward	4	quick

STEP CUE: Slow quick quick.

STYLE: In flirtation position, the dancers use the Cuban walk step, all forward or all back. The lead steps back a little larger step when he is changing to flirtation position. Finger pressure and arm control are essential as they are the only way the lead has to lead. The free arm is held up, elbow bent, parallel to the floor.

LEAD: To lead all turns, the lead dips his shoulders in the direction of the turn and his upper torso turns before his leg and foot turn. The lead's left–hand position changes to palm up, finger grasp in flirtation position. Lead may lead with fingers to push the follow backward, or to pull to bring her forward. Pressure should come on the quick beats, so that change of direction actually occurs on the next slow.

NOTE: The lead may lead as many steps in either direction as desired. To return to closed position and basic Rumba box step, the lead will be moving the follow forward in flirtation position. During a back sequence on the right foot, the lead will go into closed position as follows:

STEPS	4/4 COUNTS	RHYTHM CUE
Step R backward, pulling the follow into closed position	1–2	slow
Step L sideward, changing L-hand position	3	quick
Close R to L, roll to R	4	quick
Step L forward into the forward sequence		

SIDE BY SIDE

(Flirtation position)

Starting from flirtation position with the couple traveling either forward or backward in flirtation position, the lead turns one-quarter to the right (follow to the left), to side-by-side position, follow on the lead's left.

LEAD: On the quick quick beats, his left hand guides her into side-by-side position. She must then press with her arm against the lead's arm or wrist to follow the leads in this position. The lead may direct them forward or backward in this position, changing on the quick beats.

CIRCULAR TURN

(Side-by-side position)

Starting from side-by-side position, the couple is traveling forward. The lead on the quick beats will change his direction so as to move backward, pulling with his lead hand toward himself to direct the follow to continue forward. This will result in a turn clockwise, side by side. They should focus on each other over the shoulder.

a. Side-by-side position   ○———→   b. Circular turn
         □———→   (lead moves backward)

NOTE: The lead may return to basic box when he is on a back sequence with the right foot by facing the follow, taking Latin social position, guiding into the quick quick beats sideward left, and starting the forward sequence on the left foot.

PARALLEL TURN

(Starting from circular turn)

When traveling in circular turn, the lead backward, the follow forward, the lead on the quick beats will turn suddenly one-half counterclockwise into right parallel position and, turning clockwise, both lead and follow will be moving forward, around each other. Return to basic box as noted above.

a. Circular turn:
    lead moving backward,
    follow forward

b. Parallel turn:
    both lead and follow
    move forward

BOLERO BREAK

(Latin social position)

Starting in closed dance position, the dancers execute the forward sequence of the box step. Then, as the lead starts the back sequence, he turns the follow clockwise under his left arm. The lead continues to take the box step in place while the follow travels in a circular pattern clockwise until she faces him again at arm's distance. He has main–

tained hand contact (his left, her right) during this time and he finally guides her forward toward him back into Latin social position.

STEP CUE: Slow quick quick.

STYLE: The follow will use the Cuban walk when moving around clockwise and keep the lead's rhythm until back in closed position. She should keep the body upright, outside arm up and focus on her partner.

a.    b.

LEAD: The lead gives the lead by lifting his left hand high enough so that the follow does not have to duck her head to get under his arm. He also guides her under with his right hand. His left hand guides her around clockwise and finally draws her toward him to Latin social position.

NOTE: Any number of basic sequences (slow quick quick) may be taken, and, if the partners both keep the pattern going, they can move right back into the box step when they come together in closed position.

VARIATIONS OF BOLERO BREAK

1. *Walk Around.* As the follow comes around from Bolero break, instead of going into closed position, the lead with his left hand will lead the follow toward his right side and past his right shoulder, bringing her around behind him and toward his left side. He then turns one-half left to face her, and they move into Latin social dance position.

STEP CUE: Slow quick quick.

STYLE: The follow will use Cuban walk and keep her circle in close to the lead. The lead will keep the box step going until she passes his right side, and then he will go into the Cuban walk on a forward sequence and come around to his left to meet her. Both focus on each other. From closed position:

a. Bolero break   b. Walk around

LEAD: The lead should raise his left arm high enough so that he does not have to duck his head as the follow goes around. He will move under his own left arm and turn left to meet the follow.

NOTE: When the lead and follow meet, they should go back into Latin social position and box step on whichever foot is free.

2. *Parallel Turn.* As the follow comes around in her wide arc at arm's distance, the lead will move in toward her, coming into right parallel position, and they will turn clockwise as far as desired. The lead may then lead the follow to closed position or twirl the follow clockwise once around in place to finish in Latin social position. The lead for the twirl should come as the lead steps into the forward basic sequence with the left foot so that the follow may turn on one basic step starting with her right foot. They finish together in the back part of the box step in Latin social position.

STEP CUE: Slow quick quick.

STYLE: They use the Cuban walk. Focus on each other.

3. *Circular Turn.* Immediately after the lead turns the follow under his left arm to start the Bolero break, the lead brings his left arm down to a pressure position against the follow's right elbow and turns one–quarter right to be in a side–by–side position. Then the lead moves backward, the follow forward, turning in place clockwise. To get out of this turn, the lead turns to face the follow and steps back with his right foot into the back basic sequence, taking closed dance position.

STEP CUE: Slow quick quick.

STYLE: They must be in a tight side–by–side position. They will use the Cuban walk. Focus should be on the partner, outside arm up.

LEAD: Firmness in the arm is necessary by the lead and response to this firm pressure is needed by the follow.

VARSOUVIENNE BREAK

(Latin social position)

This is a delightful series of turns with the couple rolling from one to the other all the while keeping the basic Cuban walk rhythm, slow quick quick, going in the feet. There are four changes of position that should be practiced before the rhythm is added.

1. *Turn into the Varsouvienne position:* The lead releases the follow's right hand and reaches across in front of the lead's right shoulder to take her left hand, pulling it across in front of him, causing the follow to turn clockwise a half turn until she is by his right side, facing in the same direction. The lead now holds the follow's left hand in his left and has his right around her waist to take her right hand at her right side. They circle clockwise one complete turn. To do this effectively, the lead moves forward, the follow backward to turn in place.

2. *Turn into reverse Varsouvienne position:* The lead releases the follow's right hand and turns to his own right, bringing their joined left hands across in front of follow as she turns left until she is by his left side and slightly behind him, facing in the same direction. The follow reaches around behind him with her right hand to take his right hand at his right side. They continue to circle clockwise another complete turn, the lead now moving backward, the follow forward.

3. *Return to Varsouvienne position:* The lead releases the follow's right hand and, turning to his left, brings their joined left hands across in front of him, turning the follow halfway around clockwise until she is to the right of the lead. The lead's right arm is around her waist, holding her right hand. They continue turning clockwise, the lead again moving forward, the follow backward, one full time around.

4. *Turn back to Latin social position:* The lead releases the follow's left hand and by pulling with his right toward him he turns the follow clockwise halfway around into closed dance position. The lead changes her right hand into his left and the lead leads into the basic box step, usually on the back sequence with his right foot.

STEP CUE: Slow quick quick or change quick quick.

STYLE: Although this is described in four parts, the transitions into each part should be smooth so as to make the entire maneuver blend into one figure rather than four disconnected parts. There is no set number of Cuban walk steps to be taken for each part. The couple should turn continuously clockwise throughout the figure. Dancers should be careful to maintain good Rumba style throughout.

RUMBA COMBOS

The Rumba routines are combinations for practice, listed from simple to complex. (Latin social position, unless otherwise indicated.)

1. *Cuban Walk and Box*
   4 Cuban walks
   2 box steps
2. *Box and Bolero Break*
   2 box steps
   Bolero break
3. *Box and Flirtation Step*
   2 box steps
   flirtation break forward
   and back

4. *Bolero Break and Walk Around*
   2 box steps
   Bolero break
   walk around
5. *Bolero Break and Parallel Turn*
   2 box steps
   Bolero break
   parallel turn

6. *Flirtation Break and Reverse Turn*
   2 box steps
   flirtation break
   side by side
   parallel turn

Salsa

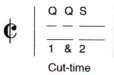ALSA MUSIC ENTERED the dance scene in the mid–1960s when the Cubans settled in Miami and southern Florida. Their Latin music became a blend of Afro–Cuban jazz. *Salsa* is the Spanish word for *sauce* and, as the Spanish sauces are spicy, the name seems appropriate.

The Salsa is written in 4/4 cut time. The rhythm is quick quick slow. It is counted 1 and 2 of the cut-time beat. The music is fast and lighthearted.

$$¢ \quad \begin{array}{c} Q \quad Q \quad S \\ - \quad - \quad - \\ \hline 1 \quad \& \quad 2 \end{array}$$
Cut-time

SALSA STYLE

The style is very similar to the rumba: bent knees, small flat footsteps (weight over the heel), hip action of the Cuban walk as it rolls, and upper body held firmly poised, never sagging, rib cage moving subtly side to side, following the action of the feet.

■ *Salsa Steps*

Directions are for the lead, follow's part reversed, except as noted.

BASIC STEP
(Latin social position)

STEPS	COUNTS	RHYTHM CUE
Step L forward	1	quick
Step R backward	*and*	quick
Step L beside R	2	slow
Step R backward	1	quick
Step L forward	*and*	quick
Step R beside L	2	slow

Use basic step to turn left or right in place.

SIDE STEP

(Latin social position)

Step sideways L	1	quick
Close R to L	*and*	quick
Step sideways L	2	slow
Reverse to R	1 *and* 2	quick, quick

CROSS STEP

(Two hands joined)

Cross L over R (with exaggeration)	1	quick
Step back R	*and*	quick
Step L close to R	2	slow

Repeat crossing right.

THROW OUT

(Latin social position)

2 Basic Steps (left right left, right left right).

Lead releases his right hand, gives the follow a slight push, and takes 2 more Basic Steps in place.

The follow moves away from partner (right, left, right) and comes back (left, right, left) to closed position.

Samba

THE *SAMBA*, FROM BRAZIL, is the most active of the Latin American dances. It was introduced to the United States about 1929. It is interesting to discover how similar it is to some of the native dance rhythms of Africa. The Samba is sensitive and smooth. The music is fiery, yet lyrical; and the dance is characterized by tiny, light footwork, and the rise and fall of the body (always turning and at the same time swaying back and forth at a most deceiving pendular angle).

SAMBA RHYTHM

Samba is written in 4/4 cut time and may be either slow or fast, although it is generally preferred at the faster tempo. The rhythm is slow quick slow, an uneven rhythm pat-tern. It has a double accent, one on each of the two major beats, and these downbeats are represented by the down movements of the dance. It will be counted as 1 *ah* 2 of the cut–time beat.

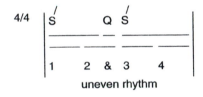

uneven rhythm

The execution of the up down weight change is the secret to the smooth, springing rhythm. There is a change of weight from one foot to the other on each of the three beats, down up down, but a preliminary uplift of the body on the upbeat of the music sets the rhythmical swing in motion. The music is fast and lighthearted.

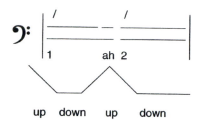

SAMBA STYLE

In contrast to the Rumba, which has a lower body movement, the Samba has a total body action. The easy springing motion comes from the ball of the foot, the flexible ankle, and the easy relaxed knees. The upper body is held firmly poised, never sagging, and it seems to sway forward and back about an axis that centers in the pelvic area. The arm, when not in contact with partner, is held out from the body, a little above waist level, bent at the elbow, parallel to the floor, palm down. The first accented step, count 1, is the largest of the three steps, the other two being like a quick–change weight step. It has been called a "step–ball–change" in the language of tap dancing. It is important to get the correct rhythm and foot pattern before working on the body sway. However, having that mastered, the body sways backward as the feet take the forward basic and forward as the feet take the back basic. Always the pattern is small and on the ball of the foot.

FUNDAMENTAL SAMBA STEPS

Directions are for the lead; the follow's part is reversed, except as noted.

BASIC STEP

(Forward and back; Latin social position)

STEPS	4/4 COUNTS	RHYTHM CUE
Step L forward	1	slow
Step R forward next to L	ah	quick
Step L in place	2	slow
Step R backward	1	slow
Step L backward beside R	ah	quick
Step R in place	2	slow

STEP CUE: Forward change weight/back change weight.

STYLE: The steps are small. Feet are close together on the change step. The rise and fall of the body begins on the upbeat with the rise of the body. This is the preparatory motion for each step. With the first step, the down motion is executed on the first slow beat, followed by an up motion on the quick beat and down again on the slow beat. The body is controlled. It does not bend at the waist.

LEAD: With the increased pressure of his right hand, the lead sways backward slightly when stepping forward with his left foot and sways forward when stepping backward with his right foot. The follow sways forward when the lead sways backward,

backward when he sways forward, so that the appearance is a rocking action parallel to each other.

■ *Samba Step Variations*

Basic Turn	Slow Side Close	Copa Step
Forward Progressive Step	Sideward Basic	

BASIC TURN

(Latin social position, counterclockwise)

STEPS	4/4 COUNTS	RHYTHM CUE
Step L forward, turning one-quarter counterclockwise	1	slow
Step R forward beside L	*ah*	quick
Step L beside R	2	slow
Step R backward, toe in, and turn one-quarter counterclockwise	1	slow
Step L backward beside R	*ah*	quick
Step R beside L	2	slow

STEP CUE: Turn step step.

STYLE: Keep the down up down motion going. Sway backward and then forward.

LEAD: Bank right arm in direction of turn, and pull into the back step.

NOTE: It is important to turn on a small base, turning on the ball of the foot, not trying to step sideward around partner.

FORWARD PROGRESSIVE STEP

(Latin social position)

STEPS	COUNTS	RHYTHM CUE
Step L forward	1	slow
Step R beside L	*ah*	quick
Step L beside R	2	slow
Step R backward, changing from closed position to two hands joined with partner	1	slow
Step L beside R	*ah*	quick
Step R beside L, drop L hand	2	slow
Into Forward Progressive Step (Side-by-side position)		
Step L forward and diagonally outward to the L (follow R)	1	slow
Step R beside L	*ah*	quick
Step L beside R	2	slow
Step R forward and diagonally inward toward partner (follow L)	1	slow
Step L beside R	*ah*	quick
Step R beside L	2	slow

Back to Latin Social Position

Step L, turning diagonally outward	1	slow
Step R beside L	ah	quick
Step L beside R	2	slow
Step R, turning diagonally inward, and take Latin social position	1	slow
Step L beside R	ah	quick
Step R beside L	2	slow
Into basic, step forward on the left foot		

STEP CUE: Forward step step change step step/out step step in step step/out step step close step step/forward step step back step step.

STYLE: The couple turns only diagonally away from each other and back, not back to back. When they come in, the outside hand, which is up turning with the body, touches partner's hand, palm to palm. Arm when free stays up.

LEAD: The lead's right hand controls the motion and the diagonal position by reaching forward and back with the hand as he turns.

NOTE: The diagonal step should reach in the line of direction each time, so that the couple will progress down the floor. The progressive step may be repeated over and over as desired.

SLOW SIDE CLOSE

(Latin social position)

A resting step.

STEPS	COUNTS	RHYTHM CUE
Step L sideward	1	slow
Close R to L, take weight R	2	slow

Repeat three times moving left. The last time, do not take weight right but be ready to go back the other direction. Take four side-close steps to the right.

STEP CUE: Side close side close.

STYLE: The sway of the Samba is discontinued as is the down up down motion. The rhythm is an even-beat step close.

LEAD: Following a basic Samba step forward and back, the lead has his left foot free. Stopping the sway and motion by control of his body and right arm, he steps left sideward into the pattern. Check lead indication 4, page 14.

NOTE: Many beginners find the Samba basic step very tiring, so this step may be used to permit the dancers a resting variation.

SIDEWARD BASIC

(Latin social position)

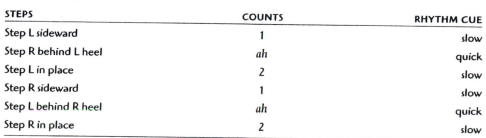

STEPS	COUNTS	RHYTHM CUE
Step L sideward	1	slow
Step R behind L heel	ah	quick
Step L in place	2	slow
Step R sideward	1	slow
Step L behind R heel	ah	quick
Step R in place	2	slow

---

b ——————→

←—————— a

Floor pattern

STEP CUE: Side back step/side back step.

STYLE: Both lead and follow may rock the body and turn the head in the direction away from the leading foot. The steps are small. A long step is awkward.

LEAD: The lead directs the sideward step with his right arm, but the body leans in the opposite direction.

NOTE: For variation, the lead may (1) turn the follow one–quarter counterclockwise as he steps to the left side, so that she turns her back on the direction they are traveling. As he repeats the step to the right, he turns her a half turn clockwise. (2) They may both turn from reverse open position to open position.

COPA STEP

(Open position)

STEPS	COUNTS	RHYTHM CUE
Step L forward	1	slow
Step R back in place on ball of foot, leaving the L foot forward	*ah*	quick
Drag L foot back half the distance, taking weight on L	2	slow
Step R forward	1	slow
Step L back in place on ball of foot, leaving R foot forward	*ah*	quick
Drag R foot back half the distance, taking weight R	2	slow

STEP CUE: Down up drag.

STYLE: The left step forward is flat with the knee bending, and the body leans backward slightly. The right step backward on the ball of the foot is accompanied by a raise of the body, which stays up during the drag of the left foot backward.

LEAD: The lead leads into the open position on the back right sequence of the basic step and then starts the copa with the left foot in open position. The lead leads the copa action by a back lean and down up up action in the body.

NOTE: Dragging the foot only halfway back allows the copa step, when repeated over and over, to progress forward in open position. If the lead opens in reverse open position, the copa will begin on the inside foot.

SAMBA COMBOS

The Samba routines are combinations for practice, listed from simple to complex. (Latin social position, unless otherwise indicated.)

1. *Basic Slow Side Close*
   8 basic (forward and backward)
   8 side close (4 left, 4 right)
2. *Basic Step and Turn*
   4 basic steps
   4 turning left
   8 side close (4 left, 4 right)
3. *Basic: Forward and Sideward*
   8 basic (forward and backward)
   4 sideward steps

4. *Basic Turn—Copa*
   4 basic turn
   4 slow side close
   4 copa steps
5. *Advanced Combo*
   4 basic
   4 sideward basic
   8 forward progressive
   8 copa steps (open)

6. *Advanced Combo*
   4 basic
   8 copa steps
   8 basic turn
   4 slow side close

7

MIXERS *and* ICE BREAKERS

MIXERS AND ICE BREAKERS

The social purposes of any dance group, be it a class or party, are greatly enriched by the use of "mixers and breakers." Ice breakers are simple line and circle dances that do not involve a partner. They are particularly useful as pre–class or pre–party warm–ups for early arrivals. Mixers provide participants an opportunity to socialize within a group. Mixers are generally designed to involve all participants en masse or in an accumulative fashion. Opening activities of this nature help establish a fun and informal atmosphere, assure quick and easy accomplishment, and add variety to the occasion.

■ *Gain or Exchange Partners*

1. **Upset the Cherry Basket:** When the music stops, the leader requests that everyone change partners. If couples are asked to change with the couple nearest them, everyone is involved, and no one walks to the side for the lack of a partner.

2. **Snowball, Whistle Dance, Pony Express, or Multiplication Dance:** One to three couples start to dance. When the music stops, each couple separates and goes to the sidelines and gets a new partner. This is repeated until everyone is dancing.

3. **Line Up:** The men line up on one side of the room, facing the wall; the women on the other side, facing the wall. When the signal is given, each line backs up until they gain a new partner.

4. **Arches:** All the dancers form a single circle and walk counterclockwise around the circle. Two couples form arches on opposite sides of the circle. When the music stops, the arch is lowered. Those caught in the arch go to the center of the circle, gain a partner, and go back to the circle to form new arches. Eventually, just a few dancers will be walking through the tunnel of arches. When all have partners, the dancing proceeds.

5. **Star by the Right:** Six men form a right–hand star in the center of a single circle formed by the group. The star moves clockwise, and the circle counter–clockwise. As the leader gives the signal, six women hook onto the star; alternate

sexes are called out until all have hooked onto the star. A little spice is added if the last person on each spoke winks or beckons a specific person from the ring to join his or her spoke. When the star is completed the woman dances with the man on her right.

6. **Matching:** Advertising slogans (Ivory Soap—99.9 percent pure, it floats), split proverbs (a rolling stone—gathers no moss), famous couples (Romeo–Juliet), pairs of words that belong together (ham—eggs), playing cards (spades match with hearts for each number, clubs with diamonds), pictures cut in half (cartoons), or songs may be used for this mixer. Half of the slips of paper are given to the men, and the corresponding halves are distributed to the women. As the people circulate, they try to find the person with the corresponding half of their slogan, proverb, cartoon, or whatever has been selected to be matched. When everyone has found his or her partner, the dancing proceeds. If songs are used, each person sings his or her song until he or she finds the person singing the same song.

7. **Musical Chairs:** Set up a double row of chairs, back to back, almost the length of the room. Leave space between every group of four chairs so that partners can get together. The group marches around the chairs. When the music stops, each person tries to gain a seat. A man must sit back to back with a woman. These two become partners and proceed to dance while all the others continue to play the game until all have partners. When all are dancing, the next signal is given and partners separate and rush for a chair, thus providing a change of partners. **Musical knees:** Played like musical chairs, except that on a signal, the men get down on one knee and the women rush to sit on a knee. Those left out go to the side.

8. **Ice Cube Pass:** Double circle with men on the outside and women on inside. Pass an orange around men's circle; an ice cube around the women's circle. When the music stops, the man with the orange and woman with the ice cube step to center of circle or its outside and become partners. Repeat over and over, until all have partners. Several oranges and ice cubes may be passed simultaneously.

9. **Mexican Broom Dance:*** As couples are dancing, an extra man with a broom knocks the broom handle on the floor several times. Partners separate, women line up on left side of man with the broom and men on right side. The two lines are about five feet part. All clap their hands while lining up and until they get a new partner. After everyone is in line, the man with the broom goes up and down the line and decides with which woman he wants to dance. When he has made his choice, he drops the broom and grabs his partner, while everyone else takes a partner too, and dancing resumes. Then the extra man picks up the broom and the procedure starts all over again. More fun is added to the mixer if the man, in going up and down the line, pretends to drop the broom but actually keeps on looking for a better partner.

■ Trade Dances

1. **Are You on the Beam?** While everyone is dancing, a spotlight is suddenly focused on a specific area. Those people standing in the rays of the light are requested to give a yell, sing a song, or trade partners.

2. **Hats Off!** Four hats are distributed among four couples. Each couple with a hat places it on one member of another couple. When the music stops, the couples with the hats must change partners.

---

*Herb Greggerson, author of *Herb's Blue Bonnet Calls*, saw this mixer danced in Mexico and presented it for the first time at a Square Dance institute at the University of Texas, April 1948. Directions were first printed in *Foot 'n' Fiddle*, Eds. Pittman, Swenson, and Sanders, 1948.

■ Tags

1. **Women's Tag or Men's Tag:** Certain dances may be designed as women's tag or men's tag.
2. **Similarity Tag:** Either a man or a woman may tag, but the person tagging can only tag someone who has a similar color of hair, eyes, shirt, shoes, and so on.
3. **"You Take the Lemon, I'll Take the Peach":** A few lemons or other designated articles are distributed among the men or the women. Anyone who holds the article may tag. Additional fun may be had by stopping the music periodically and anyone holding the article pays a forfeit. Later the forfeits are redeemed by performing a humorous stunt.

■ Elimination Dances

1. **Number Please?** Each couple is given a number. Each time the music stops, a number is called out and the couple or couples having the numbers called sit down. Numbers are called out until only one couple remains.
2. **Lemon Dance:** An object—for example, a lemon—is passed from couple to couple. When the music stops, the couple with the object sits down. Eventually one couple is left.
3. **Dance Contest:** Determine the type of dancing for the contest, for example, Waltz or Jitterbug. It should be conducted in a casual manner with qualified judges. Gradually, the contestants are eliminated until one or two couples remain. Choosing two couples, instead of one, for the winners keeps competition from becoming too keen.
4. **Orange Dance:** Each couple balances an orange or a tennis ball between their foreheads and proceeds to dance. Slow music like a Tango allows the dancers to concentrate on keeping the orange in position and still move to the music. When a couple drops the orange, they go to the sidelines. Eventually one couple is left, and the rest have enjoyed the antics of those trying to keep the orange in position. Change the rhythm of the music to match the ability of the dancers.

LINE AND CIRCLE MIXERS

Pre–class or pre–party dance activities that are set to popular music or spirited march tunes generally accommodate any number of single dancers in an accumulative fashion, thus generating a festive atmosphere to begin an occasion.

Bunny Hop

METER: 4/4. Directions are presented in beats.

MUSIC: Any schottische or music specific for Bunny Hop.

FORMATION: Single line (conga line), hands placed on waist or shoulders of dancer ahead.

(Starting with feet together, weight on both feet)

BEATS	STEPS
1–4	Hop right, touch left heel out to the side (beats 1–2), Hop right, touch left toe near right foot (beats 3–4), repeat (action is quick, quick, quick quick)
5–8	Beginning with hop on left, repeat action of beats 1–4
9–10	Jump forward (slow), weight on both feet
11–12	Jump backward (slow), weight on both feet
13–16	Take three jumps forward (quick, quick, quick, hold)

NOTE: Leader leads line in any direction around the room. Avoid cutting through other lines!

Conga

METER: 4/4. Directions presented in beats.

MUSIC: Any conga (Latin type) music.

FORMATION: Single file line, hands placed on waist of dancer ahead. (Starting feet together, weight on both)

BEATS	STEPS
1	Beginning left, step forward
2	Step right forward
3	Step left forward
4	Kick right foot to side (right knee turns in)
5	Step right forward
6	Step left forward
7	Step right forward
8	Kick left foot to side (left knee turns in)

NOTE: Leader leads line in any direction around the room. Do not travel through other lines.

Grand March

LET THE DANCE BEGIN! *Grand March* has long been a part of American dance tradition. At ceremonial occasions and balls, the instrumental groups would play a short concert prior to the dancing. Then the floor managers of the ball would signal for the dance to begin. The instrumentalists would play a march, and the couples would begin a grand promenade around the room for the Grand March. Today, for special occasions, dance festivals, and one–night stand dance parties, the Grand March is part of the program. It may not be first but perhaps after the intermission. Dancers look forward to that moment of everyone dancing together; winding in and out from one pattern to the next.

The Grand March may be used as an end in itself, since it is impressive and stimulates group feeling, or it may be used as a means for organizing a group quickly for another activity. A Grand March is most effective when many people participate. Therefore when scheduling a Grand March, consider that guests do not always arrive punctually.

MUSIC: Any lively March, Two–Step, or Square Dance tune.

POSITION: Escort.

FORMATION: Double circle, couples facing the line of direction, or single files, men in one and women in the other.

■ Leadership

The leader stands at either the front or the rear of the room. A change in pattern is indicated as the group nears the leader. It is helpful if the first two or three couples are familiar with the various figures to be used in the Grand March. Experienced couples will follow the leader's cues more easily and set the pattern for the others to follow. An assistant standing at the end opposite the leader facilitates the flow.

■ Beginning

A Grand March may be started either from two single files of individuals (particularly suited for groups not already acquainted) or in couples.

TWO SINGLE FILES

Men line up on one side of the room and women on the other. Both files face either the front or the rear of the room as indicated by the leader. Note: The leader must be careful to indicate the proper direction for the two files to face so that the women will be on the right side of the men when couples are formed. Each line marches toward the end of the room, turns, and marches toward the opposite line. The files meet, forming couples in escort position, the women to the right of the men, and march down the center of the room.

COUPLES IN A DOUBLE CIRCLE

Couples in escort position form a double circle and march counterclockwise. One couple is selected as the leader and that couple, followed by the others, moves down the center of the room.

■ Figures

These figures may be used in any order as long as they flow from one to the other.

SINGLE FILES

INNER AND OUTER CIRCLE: When each couple reaches the front of the room, partners separate, men left and women right, and travel down the side of the room until they meet at the opposite end. Then the lines pass each other. The women travel on the inside, men on the outside, and down the side of the room until they meet again at the front of the room. They pass again, the men traveling on the inside, women on the outside, and down the sides of the room.

THE CROSS (X): When each file reaches the rear corner, the leader of each file makes an abrupt turn and travels diagonally toward the front corner on the opposite side. Both files cross in the center of the room, the woman crossing in front of her partner. The files travel down the side of the room toward the rear corners. The diagonal cross is repeated, the man crossing in front of his partner.

VIRGINIA REEL: Couples move down the center in double file. When each couple reaches the front of the room, partners separate, men left, women right, and travel down the sides of the room to form two files about 10 to 15 feet apart. Both lines face each other. The head woman and the foot man meet in the middle and dance away. Then the head man and the foot woman meet in the middle in like manner and dance away. This process is repeated until all have partners and are dancing.

COUPLES

FOUR, EIGHT, OR SIXTEEN ABREAST: When the couples marching down the center arrive at the front of the room, the lead couple turns to the right, marches to the side of the room, and back toward the rear of the room. The second couple turns left, the third right, and so on, and march to the side and back to the rear of the room. When they meet at the rear of the room, the two approaching couples march down the center of the room together, thus forming a group of four abreast. At the front of the room each group of four marches alternately to the right and left, down the sides, and at the rear of the room they form a line eight abreast. The same procedure is followed to form lines of 16 or more abreast. After the group has formed lines of 16 abreast they may be instructed to mark time in place.

"RING UP" FOR SQUARES: If groups of eight are desired for the next activity, for example, a Square Dance, the couples mark time when they are eight abreast. Each line of eight then "rings up," or makes a circle.

OVER AND UNDER: When the couples are four abreast, the two couples separate at the front of the room, one turning right, the other left. When the couples meet at the rear of the room, the first couple of the double file on the right side of the room makes an arch. The first couple of the other double file goes under the arch and quickly makes an arch for the second couple they meet. All couples in both double files are alternately making an arch or traveling under an arch.

SNAKE OUT: Then the couples are 8 or 16 abreast, the person on the right end of the front line leads that line in single file to the right of the column of dancers and in between lines two and three. As the person on the left end of the first line passes the person on the right end of the second line, they join hands and line two then follows line one. The leader then leads the line between lines three and four and again as the last person in the moving line passes the right end of the third line, they join hands and line three joins with lines one and two. The moving line weaves in and out of the remaining lines and each time the person on the end of the moving line passes the right end of the next line they join hands and continue weaving in and out. After all lines have been "snaked out," the leader may lead the line in serpentine fashion around the room and eventually circle the room clockwise in a single circle, all facing the center.

DANISH MARCH: When the couples are in a double circle or double file, partners face and stand about 4 feet apart. The first couple joins hands holding arms out at shoulder height and slides the length of the formation used. The second couple follows, and so on. When couples reach the end, they join the group. This may be repeated with partners standing back–to–back as they slide.

GRAND RIGHT AND LEFT: When couples are in a single circle, partners face and start a grand right and left. This may continue until partners meet or until the leader signals for new partners to be taken for a promenade or other figure.

PAUL JONES: When couples are in a single circle, any of the figures for a Paul Jones may be used. See page 134.

■ Ending

There is no set ending for a Grand March. However, the ending should be definite so there is a feeling of completion and satisfaction. It may end with people in groups for the next activity or in a circle with everyone joining in a song or with dancers swinging into a Waltz, a Polka, or some other planned activity.

Hokey Pokey

HOKEY POKEY IS A MODERN Play Part Game popular with young and old, an adaptation of Lobby Lou. The music was written in 1947 by the Sun Valley Trio—Tafft Baker, Larry La Prise, and Charles Macak, natives of Washington. Tafft Baker wrote the words and tried them out on his girlfriend Jean. Jean and Tafft married and traveled around the United States promoting the song and dance. Acuff–Rose Opryland Music pressed the record in 1950, and the rest is history. The action sequence on several records with calls varies slightly from the one given here. The tune is simple and may easily be done without musical accompaniment. The leader may sing the call for the group or have the group sing and perform the action.

RECORDS: Can–Ed DC 74528, LS E38; Capitol 6026, EZ726; MacGregor 6995.

CASSETTE: DC 13X.

FORMATION: Single circle, individuals face center; or single circle, couples face center, follow to right of partner.

■ Call

You put your right foot in. Place foot forward into circle.

You put your right foot out. Place foot back away from circle.

You put your right foot in.

And you shake it all about. Shake foot toward center of circle.

You do the hokey pokey. Place palms together above head and Rumba hips.

And you turn yourself around. Individuals shake arms above head and turn around. If couples, lead turns follow on left 1½ with right elbow and progresses one position clockwise.

That's what it's all about. Clap hands four times.

Repeat the above call, substituting the following parts of the body: left foot, right arm, left arm, right elbow, head, right hip, whole self, backside.

■ Ending

You do the hokey pokey.

You do the hokey pokey. Raise the arms above head and lower arms and head in a bowing motion.

You do the hokey pokey. Kneel on both knees and raise arms above head and lower arms and head in a bowing motion.

That's what it's all about. Slap the floor six times.

Paul Jones Your Lady

DURING THE NINETEENTH CENTURY, the group dances with set figures, like the Quadrille, the Lancers, and the *Paul Jones*, allowed for the interchange of partners. Paul Jones, formerly danced in the ballroom and frequently used as the first dance at a party, is still danced today as a lively mixer. In some parts of the West, the same dance is called *Circle Two-Step* or *Brownee*.

MUSIC: Any lively two–step.

POSITION: Promenade.

FORMATION: Double circle, couples facing line of direction.

STEPS: Shuffle, Two–Step.

The leader calls out each figure and signals clearly. Each figure is danced briefly as it is merely a method of changing partners.

Part I: Paul Jones Your Lady or Promenade

Couples promenade around room in one large circle.

Part II: Figures

Single Circle. Couples form a single circle, hands joined. Slide left, right, and/or shuffle to center and back. Each man takes his corner woman for a new partner.

The Basket. Women form an inner circle, hands joined, and slide left. Men form an outer circle, hands joined, and slide right. Both circles stop. Men raise joined hands. Women move backward through arches made by men and stand beside a man. Men lower arms. Everyone slides left, then right. Each man takes the woman on right for a new partner.

Across the Circle. Couples form a single circle, hands joined. Slide left, right, and shuffle to center, back, and center. Each man takes the woman across the circle as a new partner.

Grand Right and Left. Couples form a single circle, hands joined. Slide left, right, and shuffle to center and back. Face partner and grand right and left around the circle. Each man takes the woman facing him or the woman whose hand he holds when leader signals for new partners.

Gentlemen Kneel. Couples form single circle and face partners. Men kneel, women move in reverse line of direction, weaving in and out between kneeling men. Each man takes the woman facing him when leader signals for new partners.

Count Off. Double circle, couples facing counterclockwise. Women stand still and men move forward, counting off as many women as indicated by leader. Men may stand still while women move forward and count off in like manner.

Part III: Two-Step

Couples in closed position, Two-Step about the room. Upon signal "Paul Jones Your Lady," they again fall into a double circle and promenade counterclockwise around room until the signal for a new figure action is given.

Patty-Cake Polka

P ATTY CAKE POLKA is a golden oldie mixer. Use a contemporary 2/4 tune. Music suggestions are listed below.

FORMATION: Double circle, lead's back to center.

STEPS: Heel and Toe Polka, slide, walk.

METER: 2/4. Directions are for lead; follow's part reverse.

(Partners face, two hands joined).

MEASURES	STEPS
	Part I: Heel and Toe Polka Slide
1–2	Beginning left, place left heel to left, place left toe to right instep; repeat
3–4	Take four slides in line of direction
5–8	Beginning right, repeat the action of measures 1–4, moving in reverse line of direction
	Part II: Claps
9	Clap own hands, clap partner's right hand
10	Clap own hands, clap partner's left hand
11	Clap own hands, clap partner's hands (both)
12	Clap own hands, slap own knees
13–14	Hook right elbows and walk around partner and back to place
15–16	Lead moves forward in line of direction to new partner; follow spins clockwise twice, as she moves in reverse line of direction to new partner
	Variation on Part II
9	Clap partner's right hand three times
10	Clap partner's left hand three times
11	Clap partner's hands (both) three times
12	Slap own knees three times

MUSIC: Medium: "If I Fall You're Going With Me," Dixie Chicks CD: *Fly*. 130 BPM; "Down On The Farm," Tim McGraw CD: *Not a Moment Too Soon*. 130 BPM
Fast: "It Doesn't Get Any Countrier Than This," Tim McGraw CD: *Not A Moment Too Soon*. 150 BPM

GLOSSARY

Accent The stress placed on a beat that makes it stronger or louder than the others. The primary accent is on the first beat of the measure. Sometimes there is more than one accent per measure. Some dance steps have the accent on the off-beat, which makes the rhythm syncopated.

Air Steps A dance move that places the follow in the air. Most often seen in Swing and Lindy hops dance styles.

Anchor Step West Coast Swing term. Step right behind left (hook) (count 1), step left in place (count *and*), step right in place (count 2). Usually danced at the end of the slot.

Arch A swing dance move where the lead lifts his left arm up (forming an arch) that either the lead or the follow can move under.

Back Break A move performed in several styles of Latin dances, where the lead steps back not forward on the break step, and releases his right hand from the follow's back.

Back Cross Position (position #1) Couple faces the same direction, the follow on the lead's right side. The lead and follow grasp right hands behind the lead's back and grasp left hands behind the follow's back.

Balance 2/4 time 1. Step left (count 1); touch right to left, rising on balls of both feet (count and); lower heels (count2); and hold (count and). Repeat, beginning right. 2. Or step left (count 1) and touch right to left (count 2). Repeat same movement, beginning right. Omit the pronounced lift of the heel in this analysis. However, there should be a slight lift of the body as the movement is executed.

Balance 3/4 time Step left (count 1); touch right to left, rising on balls of both feet (count 2); and lower heels in place (count 3). Repeat same movement beginning right. There should be a slight lift of the body, then lowering with each balance.

Banjo Position *See* Parallel Position.

Beat Basic unit that measures time. The duration of time becomes established as it is repeated.

Beguine A step from a South American dance in Bolero rhythm (2/4).

Bolero Break A dance move performed in the Rumba.

Boogie A term used to replace the word "dance" in the late 1970s through the early 1990s.

Bossa Nova A Social Dance from Brazil.

BPM Beats per minute. This is the measurement of tempo for dance music. Based upon the beats per minute, the instructor can quickly determine the best dance for a particular piece of music.

Bridge *See* Yoke Position.

Bronze Level Fundamental steps and technique used to introduce ballroom dance to beginners. Bronze steps usually finish with feet together.

Bronze Twinkle A Foxtrot dance term. A couple moves from closed position to semi open.

Butterfly Position (position #2) Couple faces, arms extended shoulder high and out to the sides, hands joined. In this position, couple may dance forward and backward or to the right or left, and in the line of direction and reverse line of direction.

Canter Rhythm An uneven pattern in 3/4 time, resulting from a long beat (counts 1–2) followed by a short beat (count 3). A step is taken on count 1 and held over on count 2. Another step is taken on count 3. The three–step turn in canter rhythm is step left (count 1); pivot on left a half–turn counterclockwise (count 2); step right (count 3), pivoting almost a half–turn counterclockwise; step left (count 1), completing the turn; and hold (counts 2–3). Close right to left (count 3), but keep weight on left. It may be done clockwise by starting with the right foot.

Centrifugal Force The force exerted outward from the center that is created by dancers rotating as in a buzz step swing or pivot turn.

Cha Cha A Social Dance from Cuba.

Challenge Position A Social Dance term. The lead faces the follow at approximately arms distance. Hands are not joined. Also called Shine position.

Charleston Step A step in 4/4 meter, accent on count *and*. Put weight on right bent knee, left foot in the air. Flip left foot up behind (count *and*); step forward left (count 1); bend left knee and flip right foot up behind (count *and*). Point right toe forward; straighten knees (count 2); bend left knee and flip right foot up behind (count *and*). Step back on right (count 3); bend right knee and flip left foot up behind (count *and*); point left toe behind and straighten knees (count 4).

Charleston Twist A variation of the Charleston.

Clockwise Refers to the movement of dancers around a circle in the same direction as the hands of a clock move or to a turning action of one dancer or couple as they progress around the floor. In directional terms, clockwise is to the left (e.g., "circle to the left").

Close Free foot is moved to supporting foot. Weight ends on free foot. Begin weight on left, move right (free foot) to left, and take weight on right.

Closed Position Partners stand facing each other, shoulders parallel and toes pointed directly forward. Lead's right arm is around the follow and the hand is placed on the small of her back. Follow's left hand and arm rest on lead's upper arm and shoulder.

Coaster Step Step back close right to left, step forward left. NOTE: An option on counts 5, 6 in Sugar Push.

Conversation Position As described for open position, but with the forward hand released and arm (lead's left, follow's right) hanging at the side.

Copa Step A dance move performed in the Samba.

Corté Social and Round dance term. *See* Dip.

Counter Balance While holding on to one or both hands, partners lean away from each other with equal force.

Counterclockwise Refers to the movement of dancers around a circle in opposite direction from the movement of the hands on a clock or to a turning action of one dancer or couple as they progress around the floor. In directional terms, counterclockwise is to the right (e.g., "circle to the right").

Couple A lead and a follow. Follow stands at lead's right.

Couple Position Partners stand side by side, follow on lead's right, inside hands joined, both facing in same direction. Also referred to as strolling, side–by–side, or open position, or inside hands joined.

Cowboy Arch (position #4) The lead lifts up his arm (forming an arch) and goes under as the follow goes behind him, trading places.

Cowboy Cross The lead lifts up both hands keeping them together, he leads the follow to his right side going under his hands, ending with arms in a "crossed position".

Cowboy Cuddle (position #7) The lead leads the follow into a cuddle, or wrap position (*see* Wrap Position).

Cross Over Position Social Dance term for Cha Cha. The couple is side by side, with inside hands joined. *See* Couple Position.

Cross Position (position #4) See Cowboy Cross.

Cuban Walk A style of walking, accenting the hips.

Cut Time A rhythm that comes from 4/4 time.

Dance Jam When a group of swing dancers form a circle and one couple at a time goes to the center to dance, sometimes showing off a special step.

Dance Walk A Social Dance term that describes the basic walking step. May move forward, backward, or sideward in Foxtrot, Waltz, or Tango.

Dip (Corté) Step back on foot indicated, taking full weight and bending the knee. The other leg remains extended at the knee and ankle, forming a straight line from the hip. The toe remains in contact with the floor.

Disco Dance A descriptive term that encompasses a wide variety of dance steps to many rhythms of recorded music. (*See* Disco Background, p. 37–38).

Discotheque A French word referring to a place where records (disques) are stored. In common usage, it describes a place for contemporary dancing to records as opposed to live music.

Escort Position Couple faces line of direction, follow to lead's right. The follow slips her left arm through the lead's right arm, which is bent at the elbow so that her left hand may rest on his right forearm. Free arm hangs to side.

Even Rhythm When the beats in the rhythm pattern are all the same value, the rhythm is said to be even.

Face Off Position A position used in the Lindy Hop. Partners are facing each other in closed position, bending slightly forward with lead's left foot forward and right foot back. Follow's footwork is opposite.

Facing Position *See* Two Hands Joined Position.

Fan A term used to describe a leadner of executing a leg motion, in which the free leg swings in a whip–like movement around a small pivoting base. Should be a small, subtle action initiated in the hip.

Flirtation Position (position #26) Also called Swing Out Position. Partners are facing; lead's left hand and follow's right hand are joined. The arms are bent and are firm so as to indicate or receive a lead.

Footwork The use of feet in the performance of dance steps.

Foxtrot An American Social Dance.

Frame Posture and tone of the upper body while in a dance position.

Funky Chicken A disco dance move, characterized by flapping the arms, like a chicken.

Funky Music Popular music from the late 1970s to the 1980s.

Gallop A basic form of locomotion in uneven rhythm moving forward diagonally with a step close, step close pattern (slow quick, slow quick).

Glide To move smoothly and continuously.

Gold Level Advanced steps and technique used in ballroom dancing.

Grapevine Step left to side (count 1), step right behind left (count 2), step left to side (count 3), and step right in front of left (count 4). Bend knees, let hips turn naturally, and keep weight on balls of feet.

Hammerlock Position (Follow will be in the Hammerlock) Partners stand side by side with right hips together, facing opposite directions. Follow's left arm is behind her back at waist level. The follow's left hand is holding on to the lead's right hand. The follow reaches in front of the lead to hold his left hand with her right. This may be reversed to put the lead in a hammerlock.

Heel Toe A disco dance move, tapping the heel, then the toe of the same foot.

Hesitation A Social Dance step that cues "step hold, step hold."

Hip Hop A style of dance developed in the 1990s (non-partner dance).

Hustle The partner dance developed during the "Disco" dance era (late 1970s).

Inside Hands Joined Position (position #11) Partners stand side by side, follow on the lead's right side, inside hands joined.

Jitterbug An American Social Dance done to jazz or swing music. *See* Lindy.

Jockey Position (position #12) Partners stand side by side in open position. Lead holds follow's right hand in his left hand at waist level. Knees are bent and couple is slightly bending over from the waist, mimicking the position of a jockey riding a horse.

Jody Position *See* Varsouvienne Position.

Jump A basic form of locomotion in which one or both feet leave the floor, knees bending; both return to the floor together; landing toe–heel with an easy knee action to catch the body weight. Spring off the floor on the upbeat of the music and land on the beat.

Ladder Refers to a step that moves sideward, then forward, sideward, forward as in the Merenque.

Latin Social Position (position #13) Partners are in closed position with lead's left elbow touching the follow's right elbow.

Lead A physical signal to alert the follow of the next move.

Left Parallel Position *See* Parallel Position.

Lindy An American Social Dance done to jazz or swing music in 4/4 or cut time. There are three Lindy rhythms—single, double, and triple.

Lindy Hop An American Social Dance first done in the late 1920s in Harlem.

Line A type of formation. Dancers stand side by side, all facing in the same direction.

Little Window Position (position #15) Partners stand side by side with right hips together, facing opposite directions. Right arms are in front with a 90° bend at the elbow. The elbow is next to the partner's shoulder. Partners hold right hands on top and shake left hands in the window created by the right arm.

Magic Step A Social Dance term. A basic step of the American Foxtrot.

Measure One measure encloses a group of beats made by the regular occurrence of the heavy accent. It represents the underlying beat enclosed between two adjacent bars on a musical staff.

Meter Refers to time in music or group of beats to form the underlying rhythms within a measure.

Note Values A term used to refer to the relative value of the musical notes or beats that make up the rhythmic pattern

Octopus Position (position #16) With two hands joined, partners stand side by side with right hips together, facing opposite directions. The lead's hand is behind his head and right hand is behind his partner's head.

Open Position (position #17) Partners stand side by side, follow on lead's right, facing in the same direction. Lead's right arm is around follow's waist. Follow's left hand rests on lead's right shoulder. Lead holds follow's right hand in his left. Arms extend easily forward.

Parallel Position Refers to right or left parallel position. Right parallel is a variation of closed position, in which both lead and follow are turned one-eighth turn counterclockwise to a position facing diagonal. The follow is slightly in front of but to the right of the lead. Also referred to as banjo position. In left parallel position, lead and follow are turned clockwise to face diagonally on the other side. Follow is in front of and to the left of the lead.

Partner Follow to immediate *right* of lead and lead to immediate *left* of follow.

Phrase A musical term that represents a short division of time comprising a complete thought or statement. In dance, it is a series of movements considered as a unit in a dance pattern. It is a group of measures, generally 4 or 8, but sometimes 16 to 32.

Pigeon Wing Position Lead and follow face each other and place their right forearms, held vertically, close together. The palms are held together, open and upright, and elbows are almost touching.

Pivot Turn clockwise or counterclockwise on balls of one or both feet.

Pivot Turn Closed or shoulder-waist position. Step left, pivoting clockwise (count 1), continuing in same direction step right (count 2); step left (count 3), and step right (count 4). Make one complete turn progressing in line of direction. May also be done counterclockwise.

Pressure Lead A lead in which extra pressure is exerted by the fingers, arm, or body in order to lead the follow into a particular position or step.

Pretzel A three-part move that is usually done in Cowboy Swing.

Promenade Position, Ballroom Style Semiopen position in the Foxtrot and Tango is often referred to as Promenade.

Push Step Moving to the left, beginning left, step (chug) to the side (count 1); bring right toe close to left instep; and push right foot away from body (count *and*). Repeat pattern. The push step is similar to a buzz step, except that the action is taken to the side instead of in a turning or circling movement.

Q Symbol for Quick. Used for Rhythm Cue. For example, QQSS, Quick Quick Slow Slow.

Quick A rhythm cue. For example, 4/4 time, 4 quarter beats to each measure; each beat is given the same amount of time, an accent on the first beats of the measure. When a step is taken on each beat (1–2–3–4), these are called *quick* beats. When steps are taken only on 1 and 3, they are twice as long and are called *slow* beats.

Reverse Open Position (position #20) From an open Social Dance position, facing line of direction, partners turn in toward each other to face reverse line of direction but do not change arm or hand positions.

Reverse Varsouvienne Position (position #21) Couples are standing almost side by side, with the follow on the left side of the lead. She is slightly behind him. The lead reaches across in front of the follow to hold her left hand in his left. Her right arm is around his shoulders and her right hand grasps his right hand at shoulder level. For Social Dance, the right arm is sometimes extended behind partner at waist level and grasps his hand at the waist. Still a different concept of reverse Varsouvienne position is merely to turn half about from Varsouvienne position. Now the follow is on lead's left side but slightly in front of him, and his left arm is around her shoulders. Her right arm is across in front of him.

Rhythm Pattern The rhythm pattern in dance is the grouping of beats for the pattern of a dance step. The rhythm pattern must correspond to the underlying beat of the music.

Right Parallel Position *See* Parallel Position.

Rock A dance term used when the dancer steps forward (or backward) a short step and then backward (or forward) a short step. With the body weight shifting forward and backward over the foot, this creates a rocking motion. The term is used in Social Dance and in American Round Dance and Folk Dance.

Rock-and-Roll When the second and fourth beats are accented in country western and folk blues music, it is referred to as rock-and-roll music. Contemporary fad dances are done to rock-and-roll music. Rock-and-roll is a rhythm; but the term *Rock Dance* is used.

Rumba A Latin American Dance from Cuba in 4/4 time.

Running Waltz A step used in European Folk Dance. Take three tiny running steps with the accent on the first beat, three beats to each measure.

S Symbol for slow. Used for Rhythm Cue. *See* Quick.

Samba A Latin American Dance from Brazil in 4/4 or cut time.

Semiopen Position (position #23) A Social Dance position halfway between open and closed position.

Shine Position A Social Dance term. The lead faces the follow at approximately arms distance. Hands are not joined. Also called the Challenge Position.

Shoulder-Waist Position (position #24) Partners stand facing each other, toes pointed directly forward. The lead extends his arms, rounded, and places his hands below the follow's shoulder blades. The follow places her arms gently on the lead's arms, her hands folding over the lead's shoulder. The follow supports the weight of her arms and gives a firm pressure with her hands. Both lean slightly away from each other against the firm hand support of the other.

Shuffle An easy, light walking step (one step), with the ball of the foot kept lightly in contact with the floor as they move, in even rhythm.

Side Car Position *See* Parallel Position.

Silver Level Intermediate steps and technique used in ballroom dancing. Silver steps are progressive, constantly traveling in line of direction.

Skip A basic form of locomotion in uneven rhythm. The pattern is a step and a hop on the same foot in slow quick slow quick rhythm.

Slide A basic form of locomotion in uneven rhythm. The movement is sideward. It is a step close, step close pattern (slow quick slow quick).

Slot Dance The West Coast Swing is referred to as a slot dance because couples move forward and backward in a narrow space.

Slow A rhythm cue. *See* Quick.

Social Swing Position A Social Dance position similar to "semiopen", with the lead's left palm up and the follow's right palm down, these arms lowered.

Step Close Step sideward left (count 1), and close right to left, take weight on right (count 2). The right foot does not draw along the floor, but moves freely into place beside left.

Strut Walk forward, upper torso high and leading, left knee slightly bent, toe pointed, preparing to step. Step on *ball of foot first* and then lower heel gently.

Sugar Push A variation of West Coast Swing.

Suzy Q Moving sideward, toes are together, heels apart, "pigeon toes." Weight on both feet, shift weight to left heel, right toe simultaneously, pivoting to "pigeon toe" position; shift weight to left toe, right heel, pivoting to toes out, "roach toe." Alternating toe heel, heel toe, move sideward. Also called Swivel.

Sweetheart Position (position #28) Country Western dance position. Same as the Varsouvienne position.

Swing Out Position See Flirtation position.

Swivel Toes and heels move sideward, either weight on toes, pivoting heels, or weight on heels, pivoting toes. Also called Suzy Q. Or, pivoting on one toe and one heel simultaneously, then pivoting on the other toe and heel, alternating toe heel, heel toe, moving sideward; or, in place by shifting weight, feet are "pigeon-toed," then heels together, toes pointed out "roach toe."

Swivel Turn In one spot, a complete turn on the ball of one foot, either direction. Free foot may be lifted, bending knee, or close to other heel.

Syncopation A temporary displacement of the natural accent in music. For instance, shifting the accent from the naturally strong first and third beat to the weak second and fourth beat.

Tango A Latin American dance from Argentina.

Tempo Rate of speed at which the music is played, or the speed of the dance.

Throw Out A move in the hustle, where the lead sends the follow from closed position to swing out position.

Time Signature A symbol indicating duration of time. Example: In 2/4 time, the upper number indicates number of beats per measure, while the lower number indicates the note value that receives one beat.

Tone Firm, yet not resistance, state of muscles while dancing.

Traveling Box Using the basic waltz box step to travel forward in line of direction.

Triple Rhythm Used in East Coast Swing. Three little steps to each slow beat, similar to a fast two–step.

Triple Time Swing Step Used in East Coast Swing.

Turning Basic (collegiate) A Swing Dance term. Rotating clockwise, while performing the basic single time step.

Twinkle Step A variation based on box rhythms for both Foxtrot and Waltz.

Two Hands Joined Position (position #27) Partners stand facing each other, shoulders parallel, and toes pointed directly forward. Two hands are joined, lead's palms up, his thumbs on top of her hands. The elbows are bent and held close to the body.

Two–Step Step left (count 1), close right to left (count 2), step left (count 3), and hold (count 4).

Underarm Pass A West Coast Swing Dance Term. The follow moves under the lead's arm passing next to him.

Underlying Beat The duration of time becomes established by the beat or the pulse. As the beat is repeated, it is referred to as the underlying beat.

Uneven Rhythm When the beats in the rhythm pattern are not all the same value but are a combination of slow and quick beats, the rhythm is said to be uneven.

Varsouvienne Position (position #28) Couple faces in line of direction, follow in front and slightly to the right of lead. Lead holds follow's left hand in his left at shoulder level. Lead's right arm extends back of follow's shoulders and holds follow's raised right hand in his right. In Social Dance, this is sometimes called Jody Position.

Walk A basic form of locomotion in even rhythm. Steps are from one foot to the other, the weight being transferred from heel to toe.

Walk Through/Brush Off A Swing Dance term. In Two Hand position, the lead releases his right hand and moves to his left, turning his back to the follow. The lead releases his right hand to pass through the follow's left arm. The lead rejoins his right hand to the follow's left hand.

Waltz Step forward left (count 1), step sideward right (count 2), close left to right, and take weight left (count 3).

Waltz Balance *See* Balance, 3/4 time.

Westchester Box Step A Foxtrot move that is based on slow, quick, quick rhythm in 4/4 time.

Whip A variation of West Coast Swing.

Wrap Position (position #7) The follow is at the right of the lead. His right arm is around her waist and his hand holds her left hand. His left hand is holding her right hand in front. Same as Cuddle Position.

Yoke Position (position #29) Couple is standing side by side with the follow on the right side of the lead. Lead holds follow's left hand in his left hand, behind his shoulder. Lead's right arm extends back of follow's shoulders and holds follow's raised right hand in his right hand.

PERIODICALS

Amateur Dancers The official membership publication of the United States Ballroom Dancers Association, Inc. Editorial Offices: Robert Meyer, Editor East, 1427 Gibsonwood Rd., Baltimore, MD 21228, Phone and Fax: (410) 747–7855. Joan Adams, Editor West, 16755 Wallingford Avenue North, Seattle, WA 98133. Phone and Fax: (206) 542–1639.

Ballroom Dancing Times Clerkenwell House, 45–47 Clerkenwell Green, London, England ECIR OEB.

Country Dance Lines (Country Western) P.O. Drawer 139, Woodacre, CA 94973; Phone: (415) 488–0154.

Dancesports Magazine P.O. Box 13, Boca Raton, FL 33429

Dancing USA 10600 University Avenue N.W., Minneapolis, MN 55448–6166. Phone: (612) 757–4414. Fax (612) 757–6605.

ORGANIZATIONS AND RESOURCES

Ballroom Dance Camps, Conferences, and Workshops. 155 Harman Building, Brigham Young University, Provo, UT 84602. Phone: (801) 378–4851.

College Ballroom Dance Association. Newsletter, editor: Suzanne Zelnik-Geldys, HPERD 116 Warner Hall, Eastern Michigan University, Ypsilanti, MI 48197. Phone: (313) 487–4388.

Henry Neeman's List contains a little bit of everything. Contests cover: General Dance Resources, General Partner Dance Resources, Ballroom Dance-Dancesport, Swing & Night Club Dance, Argentine Tango, Salsa Dance, Country-Western Partner and Line Dances, Miscellaneous Partner Dances, Non-Partner Dance Resources, Dance Music Resources, Supplies and Services, Usenet Newsgroups.

McDonagh, D. (1979) *DANCE FEVER*, New York: Random House. National Endowment for the Arts (NEA) & U.S. Department of Education (1994). Arts education research agenda for the future. Washington, D.C.: U.S. Government Printing Office.

National Teachers Association of Country & Western Dance Ms. Kelly Gillette, President, 1817 Lamp Lighter Lane, Las Vegas, NV 89104.

United States Amateur Ballroom Dancers Association Inc. Youth-College Network, P.O. Box 128, New Freedom, PA 17349. **Editor East:** Robert Meyer, 1427 Gibsonwood Road, Baltimore, MD 21228 Phone and Fax: (410) 747–7855. **Editor West:** Joan Adams, 16755 Wallingford Avenue North, Seattle, WA 98133. Phone and Fax: (206) 542–1639.

WORLD WIDE WEB ADDRESSES

Gives general information and other dance links. Many have a sales section with instructional videos and music.

Ballroom www.dancescape.com
www.ballroomdancers.com

Swing & Lindy Hop www.ltdance.com
www.thejointisjumpin.com
www.pasadenaballroomdance.com

MUSIC AND INSTRUCTIONAL AIDS

Music for Social Dance or Ballroom Dance is subject to the particular "sound" in vogue at a particular point in time. "Standards" are tunes that are recognized by musicians and the public alike as favorites and do, indeed, survive several generations. At present, music for dancing is available in the form of CDs, cassettes, and videos. Sources listed under "General" carry some, if not all, types of music listed.

GENERAL

A Muse-A-Mood Co., 128 Hancock Place NE, Leesburg, VA 22075. Audio-Visual Catalogue, books, manuals, instructional tapes, and videos. Booklets covering dance steps (beginners to advanced), history of swing, and music fundamentals.

Dance Vision USA, 4270 Cameron Street, Ste. 3A, Las Vegas, NV 89103. Phone: 1 (800) 851–2813, Fax: 1 (702) 365–6644. Catalogue of instructional videos, tapes, and CDs.

Living Traditions, 2442 NW Market St, #168, Seattle, WA 98107, Phone: (206) 781–1238 or 1 (800) 500–2364. Source for videos, CDs, and cassettes.

Tango Catalogue, B–2, Juniper East, Yarmouth, ME 04096–1439. The catalogue features: The Best of Tango Video Series; Daniel & Rebecca's Instructional Video; Argentine Master Teachers on Video; Tango music and CDs; Cassettes; Tango Books and other products. A 1997 tour to Buenos Aires to explore the Tango in its home setting.

Tower Records, Phone: 1 (800) ASK TOWER.

CDS AND CASSETTES

Dance Plus, 2018 Granby Drive, Oakville, Ontario, Canada, L6H 3X9; Phone: (905) 849–4122, Fax (905) 849–7085. Over 500 strict time ballroom CDs. New releases and music list available.

Dance Trax International, CDs for International style, American style, and showcase dancing. 2217 N. Woodbridge, Saginaw, MI 48602; Phone and Fax (517) 799–0349; Orders: (800) 513–2623.

Ewers and Mine Software, CD-ROM multimedia interactive dance instruction. 3702 S.W. Court Avenue, Ankeny, IA 50021.

Lane, Christy, National Dance Association. Attention: Millie Pucci. 1900 Association Drive, Preston, VA. 20191–1598. Complete Party Dance Music on CD.

Living Traditions, 2442 N.W. Market Street, #168, Seattle, WA 98107; (206) 781–1238; Phone: (800) 500–2364. *Roll up the Rug,* Triple Swing, Volume I and II, and Rhythm and Blues. *Really Swingin',* Frankie Mannings "Big Band Favorites." *Cascade of Tears,* 15 Romantic Dances. Popular Vintage Dances. Cajun Music. Zydeco Music.

Musical Services, 409 Lyman Avenue, Baltimore, MD 21212; Phone: (800) 892–0204; Fax (410) 433–7948. Helmut Licht—Variety of cassettes and CDs of ballroom favorites.

Pro Dance, Suite 201, 1152 Victoria Street, Lemoyne, QC, J4R 1R1, Canada. CDs for class practice or home use all in international dance rhythm (BPM).

VIDEOS

Allons Danser! Randy Speyrer, P.O. Box 15908, New Orleans, LA 70175–5908. Phone: (504) 899–0615. "Cajun Dancing" step–by–step instruction. Waltz, Two–Step, One–Step, Cajun Jitterbug.

B & M Dance Productions (AD). 6804 Newbold, Bethesda, MD 20817 American Social Dance instructional videos for beginners to advanced. "How To" tapes teach beginners to advanced steps.

Best Film and Video Corp., Great Neck, NY 11021. "Fred Astaire Dancing: Ballroom (Foxtrot, Waltz), Latin (Cha Cha, Salsa)."

Brentwood House Video, 5740 Corsa Ave., Suite 102, Westlake Village, CA 91362. "Line Dancing," "New Line Dancing," "Fun and Funky Freestyle Dancing," "Line Dancing Vol. 2," Christy Lane.

Coffey Video Productions. 3300 Gilbert Lane, Knoxville, TN 37920. Phone: (800) 423–1417, "Texas Two Step."

Dance America. Dance Basics Plus Ballroom Dancing I. Intermediate Level, Single Time, East Coast Swing, 30 minutes.

Dance Lovers. P.O. Box 7071, Ashville, NC 28802. VHS videos, music, and tapes.

Dancing Times Limited, 45–47 Clerkenwell Green, London, EC1R OEB. Extensive stock of ballroom Dancing Times books and videos.

Hoctor Products for Education. P.O. Box 38, Waldwick, NJ 07463. Phone: (201) 652–7767, Fax: (201) 652–2500. "Hip Hop," "Charleston."

Human Kinetics, P.O. Box 5076, Champaign, IL 61825–5076. Social Dance Music Set, Item MGAR0l91. Individual tapes cover Swing, Waltz, Cha Cha, Foxtrot, and Polka music.

J. Henley. Livonia, MI. 1987. Discover the Magic of Social Dancing.

Kultur. West Long Branch, NJ. 1999. Wedding Dances: easy lessons for your special dance. Video 70 minutes: Waltz, Tango, Foxtrot, Rumba, Cha Cha.

Lane, Christy. Complete Guide to Party Dances. New video of most requested party dances. Electric Slide, YMCA, Macarena, Chicken Dance, Stroll, Conga, Hand Jive, Swing. National Dance Association. Attention: Millie Puccio, 1900 Association Drive, Reston, VA 20191–1598.

Let's Do It Productions. Westlake Village, CA. 1998 Christy Lanes' Surviving the Country Dance Floor. Video 50 minutes.

Let's Do It Productions, P.O. Box 5483, Spokane, WA 99205. Phone: (509) 235–6555. Fax: (509) 255–4445. Line Dance, Country Western videos and manuals.

Living Traditions, Phone: (206) 781–2238 or 1 (800) 500–2364. Savoy–style Lindy Hop, Levels 1,2, 3. Instructional video.

Living Traditions, Phone: (206) 781 –2238 or 1 (800) 500–2364. Shim Sham (instructional video) Swing, etc. from 1930s and 1940s.

Marshall & Lawrence and Associates, Memphis, TN. 1998. Catch Dance Fever with Alan Meyers. #7 1998, #8 1999. Video 60 minutes. Foxtrot, Waltz, Cha Cha.

Nancy Hays Entertainment, Chicago, IL. 1999. Bring Back the Romance of Dance. Tango, Waltz. Video 48 minutes. Author: Hays and Gale.

_____, Chicago, IL. 1999. Jitterbug, Lindy, Charleston, Swing. Video 59 minutes. Romance of Dance Series.

_____, Chicago, IL. 1999. Bring Back the Romance of Dance. Volume 2: Tango and Waltz. Video 48 minutes. 1997.

Volume 3: Beginning Rumba, Cha Cha, Salsa. Video 40 minutes.

National Association of Country Dances, P.O. Box 9841, Colorado Springs, CO 80932. "28 Country Swing Moves and Combinations."

Not Strictly Ballroom. Vance Productions c/o Colortech Video Productions, 4501 College Blvd, Ste 110, Shawnee Mission, Kansas 66211–9989. The first complete Social Dance Library of Videotapes. Beginning, Intermediate and Advanced Series: Covers: Foxtrot, Waltz, Tango, Viennese Waltz, Rumba, Cha Cha, East Coast Swing, Samba, Mambo, Merengue, West Coast Swing, Country Western Dances: Two–Step, Waltz, Polka, Cha Cha, Eastern Swing, Western Swing, Country Line dances, the "B.C." (8 tapes in all).

Parade Video. 1998. Cal Pozo's Learn to Dance in Minutes. Video 50 minutes. Swing, Foxtrot, Waltz, Lindy.

PPI Entertainment—Parade Video. Newark, NJ. 1998. Foxtrot, Waltz, Lindy.

PPI Parade Video, 88 St. Francis St., Newark, NJ 17105. "Texas Dance Styles"" by Valerie Moss and Scott Schmitz; "Texas Two–Step," "Down and Dirty" (Jerk, Twist, Stroll, Monkey, Hustle, etc.).

Princeton Book Co. 12 West Delaware Avenue, Pennington, NJ 08534. Phone: 1 (800) 220–7149, Fax: (609) 737–1869. "Author Murray Dance Magic Series." Waltz, Tango, Swing, Samba, Merengue, Night Club, Rumba, Salsa, Cha Cha, Dancin' Dirty, Foxtrot, Mambo. (50 minutes).

_____, Jitterbug: Beginners (Kyle Webb and Susan Parisi). East Coast Swing, West Coast Swing. (60 minutes).

_____, Jitterbug: Intermediate (Kyle Webb and Susan Parisi). More stylish moves, East and West Coast Swing. (60 minutes).

_____, "Sex and Social Dance." Social dance history, clips of Astaire and Rogers, rock and roll, Elvis, twist, disco scenes. (Box of 8 tapes, 60 minutes each).

Quality Video Inc., 7399 Bush Lake Road, Minneapolis, MN 55439. "Country Line Dancing for Kids," "Country Line Dancing," "More Country Line Dancing." (Diane Horner).

R & R Video International Dancing in America Series. 3649 Whittier Blvd., Los Angeles, CA 90023. "West Coast Swing." (Skippy Blair).

Sigma Leisure. Wilmslaw, Cheshire, England. Salsa and Merenque: The Essential Step by Step Guide. 1999. Video 30 minutes.

Simitar Entertainment, Maple Plain, MN. Two videos: 95 minutes. Tape 1: Learn the History. Tape 2: Learn the Moves. Ballroom, Disco, Jitterbug.

Simitar Entertainment, Maple Plain, MN. Tape 1: West Coast Swing and L.A. Hustle. Tape 2: East Coast Swing and Jitterbug.

Supreme Audio, Inc. P.O. Box 50, Marlborough, NH 03455, Phone: (800) 445–7398; Fax: (603) 876–4001. Large collection of Square, Clogging, Country Western, Texas, East Coast Swing, and West Coast Swing videos.

Tanguero Productions, 5351 Corteen Place, code ADL1, North Hollywood, CA 91607. Alberto Toledano and Loreen Arbus "Tango–Argentine Style" instructional video.

Universal, CA. Burn the Floor. 1999. Recording for Hearing Impaired. Author: Jason Roditis.

BIBLIOGRAPHY

Akrill, Ken. *The Social Dance Survival Guide.* Ballroom and Disco dancing. Sigma Leisure: Wilmslaw, Cheshire. 1998

Bottner, Paul. *Dance Crazy Series.* Quick Step, Waltz, American Line, Rock 'n' Roll, Salsa. Lorenz Books. New York, NY, 10011. (800) 354–9657.

Bottomer, Paul. *Line Dancing.* New York: Anness Publishers, 1996.

Collier, Simon, Artenis Cooper, Maria Susana Azzi, and Richard Martin. *Tango, The Dance, The Song, The Story.* London: Thames & Hudson Ltd., 1995.

Duke, Jerry. *Social and Ballroom Dance Lab Manual,* San Francisco: Duke Publishing Co., 1988.

Elfman, Bradley. *Breakdancing.* New York: Avon Books, 1984.

Ericson, Jane Harris and Diane Ruth Albright. *File O' Fun,* 3d ed., 1996. File cards for Mixers, Musical Mixers, Line Dances and Novelty Dances–cards. Venture Publishing Co. Inc. 1999 Cato Ave., State College, PA 16801.

Fischer–Munstermann, Uta. *Jazz Dance and Jazz Gymnastics Including Disco Dancing.* New York: Sterling Publishing Co., Inc., 1978.

Greggerson, Herbert S., *Herb's Blue Bonnet Calls,* Cameo Lodge, Box A, Ruidoiso, New Mexico, 1946. Hager, Steven. *Hip Hop: The Illustrated History of Break Dancing, Rap, Music, and Graffiti.* New York: St. Martin's Press, 1984.

Hampshire, Harry Smith, and Doreen Casey. *The Viennese Waltz.* Brooklyn, NY: Revisionist Press, 1993.

Heaton, Alma. *Disco with Donny and Marie, Step by Step Guide to Disco Dancing.* CA and MT: Osmond Publishing Co., Provo, UT. 1979.

——. *Techniques of Teaching Ballroom Dance.* Promo, UT: Brigham Young University Press. 1965.

——. *Techniques of Teaching Ballroom Rhythms.* Dubuque, IA: Kendall/Hunt Publishing Co., 1971.

——. *Fun Dance Rhythms.* Provo, UT: Brigham Young University Press, 1976.

Heaton, Alma, and Israel Heaton. *Ballroom Dance Rhythms.* Dubuque, IA: William C. Brown Co., 1961.

Hostetler, L. A. *Walk Your Way to Better Dancing,* A.S. Barns and Company, New York, Revised 1952.

Javna, John. *How to Jitterbug.* New York: St. Martin's Press, 1984.

Laird, Walter. *Technique of Latin Dancing: International Dance.* London: Book Service. New edition 1988. Reprint 1992.

——. *The Ballroom Dance Pack.* London: Dorling Kindersley. Publisher: Houghton Mifflin Co., 1994.

Lane, Christy. *Complete Book of Line Dancing.* Champaign, IL, Human Kinetics, 1995.

Livingston, Peter. *The Complete Book of Country Swing and Western Dance and a Bit About Cowboys.* Garden City, NY: Doubleday & Co., Inc., 1981.

Lustgarten, Karen. *The Complete Guide to Disco Dancing.* New York: Warner Books, Inc., 1978.

Marlow, Curtis, *Break Dancing.* Cresskill, NJ: Sharon Publications, Inc., 1984.

Monte, John. *The Fred Astaire Dance Book.* New York: Simon and Schuster, 1978.

Moore, Alex. *Ballroom Dancing: with 100 Diagrams and Photographs of the Quickstep, Waltz, Foxtrot, Tango.* London: A & C Clark Publisher, 1986.

Murray, Author, *How to Become a Good Dancer,* Simon and Schuster, New York, Revised 1954.

National Association of Country Dancers. *Country and Western Dance Manual.* P. O. Box 9841, Colorado Springs, CO 80932.

Osborne, Hilton. *Line Dancing: Run to the Floor for Country Western.* Glendale, CA: Griffin Publisher, 1994.

Pittman, Anne, Marlys Swenson and Olcutt Sanders (Eds.). *Foot 'n' Fiddle,* May 1948.

Ray, Ollie Mae. *Encyclopedia of Line Dances.* Reston, VA: National Dance Association, American Alliance for Health, Physical Education, Recreation and Dance, 1992.

Rushing Productions, 5149 Blanco Rd., #214, San Antonio, TX 78216. *Kicker Dancin' Texas Style.* How to do the top ten Country and Western Dances like a Texas cowboy, 1982.

Rushing, Shirley. *Ballroom Dance American Style.* Eddie Bowers Pulishing, Inc. Dubuque, IA. 1997.

Sarver, Mary J. 1224 SW Normandy Terrace, Seattle, WA 98166. *"Pattern Ballroom Dances for Seniors,"* 27 dances, 1992.

Schild, Myrna Martin. SIU Box 1126, Edwardsville, IL 62026. *"Smooth Dances"* (Foxtrot, Waltz, Tango), *"Rhythm Dances"* (Polka and Regional Dances, Samba, Merengue, Swing, Mambo, Cha Cha and Rumba).

Selmon, Simon. *Let's Lindy*. UK,: Princeton Book Co., 12
West Delaware Avenue, Pennington, NJ 08534, 1993.

Smiley, Patricia. *Ballroom Dance Guide*—First Steps Counting
5, 6, 7, 8. Dendall Hunt. 1998.

Spencer, Peggy. *The Joy of Dancing*. Chameleon Books,
Andre Deutsch, LTD. 106 Great Russel Street, London,
WCIB3LJ. 1997.

Spencer, Peggy. *The Joy of Dancing The Next Steps*. Chameleon
Books, Andre Deutsch, LTD. 106 Great Russel Street,
London, WCIB3LJ. 1999.

Stephenson, Richard M., and Joseph Iaccarino. *The Complete Book of Ballroom Dancing*. New York: Doubleday,
1980.

Thorpe, Edward. *Black Dance*. New York: Overlook Press,
1989, reprint 1994.

Veloz and Yolands. *Tango and Rumba*. New York: Harper
and Brothers, 1939.

Wagner, Michael. "Swing Dance," *Viltis*, September/Octo–
ber 1997.

Wainwright, Lyndon B. *First Steps to Ballroom Dancing*. 66 B
The Broadway, Mill Hill, London NW 7 3TF, England:
Lyric Books Limited, 1993.

Wright, Judy Patterson. *Social Dance: Steps to Success*. Leisure
Press a division of Human Kinetics, P.O. Box 5076,
Champaign, IL: Leisure Press, 1992.

DANCE INDEX

SUBJECT INDEX